*Perform It!*

# Perform It!

A Complete Guide to Young People's Theatre

## Jan Helling Croteau

HEINEMANN
Portsmouth, NH

**Heinemann**
A division of Reed Elsevier Inc.
361 Hanover Street
Portsmouth, NH 03801–3912
www.heinemanndrama.com

*Offices and agents throughout the world*

CIP data is on file with the Library of Congress.
ISBN: 0-325-00230-4

Editor: Lisa A. Barnett
Production coordinator: Sonja Chapman
Production service: Melissa L. Inglis
Cover design: Catherine Hawkes/Cat and Mouse
Manufacturing: Deanna Richardson

Printed in the United States of America on acid-free paper
04   03   02   01   00   DA      2   3   4   5

*I dedicate this book
with love to
Richard, Maggie, and Hannah.
I will be forever grateful
that you are my family.*

*And
to the students
and their families,
past, present, and future
of Encore Young People's Stage Company*

# Contents

# Preface: One Bite at a Time

Confidence is the most important gift that the performing arts offers to young people. Stage work is a dynamic, creative expression that can transform children into motivated and enthusiastic individuals. Its power and intensity changes them right to the core of their being. Through theatre work, young people are given the opportunity to discover their strengths and capabilities, which results in self-assurance.

This book grew out of my experiences as a theatre director and teacher. There are activities, ideas, and step-by-step production notes, presented in a user-friendly manner that a novice can follow. While at first, developing a comprehensive theatre program for young people can seem like an overwhelming project, taking it one step at a time is the key to success.

I once met a well-known woman who had accomplished a great deal in her life. When I asked her how she had done it, she replied, "It's like eating an extravagant gourmet twelve-course meal. You just take it one bite at a time." I hope this book will help you to break down the enormously satisfying meal of theatre production into bite-size pieces, and will encourage you to discover the tremendous inspiration and empowerment theatre work can bring to people of all ages . . . especially young people.

# Acknowledgments

Like a good theatre production, writing a book is the collaborative effort of many talented individuals.

First I would like to thank my daughters, Maggie and Hannah, for their love and belief in my work; without them I would never have started Encore Young People's Stage Company. Deep appreciation for and love to my husband, Richard, who has encouraged my creativity since the day we first met and has fostered an environment of growth and exploration in everything we do.

A debt of gratitude goes out to my sister-in-law, close friend, and loving supporter, freelance editor Aysha Griffin. Her work on my behalf has helped make this book a success. It is your turn next, Aysh.

To my brother, David Helling, for believing in me always, and to my parents, Margaret and William Helling, for helping me with the manuscript and giving me a strong family foundation.

A special thanks to all the young people of Encore who have been so willing and eager to work with me as a theatre director. Your youth and vitality, your honesty and sincerity, guide my way. May we produce many more quality productions together and may our dream of owning our own theatre become a reality someday.

I am also grateful to Donna Powell, Marybeth Wadlinger, and Julie Way for their effort in keeping our theatre group alive and supporting the writing of this book. It is a pleasure to work with women of such integrity, who make board meetings so much fun.

I would like to thank my dear friend Sarah Lukas for making so many things possible for me through her love and generosity, and Kitty Leaken for her thoughtful suggestions and comments concerning the manuscript.

Although I have never met her, I thank Linda Weise, founder and director of the Colorado Springs Conservatory, for taking the time to read and make suggestions on the first manuscript; may

we meet soon. To Diane Ducret for her insights and encouragement. And to Tim Scannell for his generosity and patience.

A special thanks to Lisa Barnett, senior editor, at
Heinemann, for her help in putting this book into your hands.

# Introduction: Encore Young People's Stage Company: "All the World's a Stage"

"We want to be in a play!" my daughters stated emphatically.

As a homeschooling family, we were used to being creative in finding resources in our area. Our small New England community offered few opportunities for aspiring young thespians. Ignorance being bliss, I thought that the idea of starting a theatre group for young people was something I could handle.

When I attended college in the early 1970s, my major was fine art, with a minor in theatre. I always loved theatre, had a small amount of experience in it, and thought I could tackle the project. Little did I know how the rather bold step into the world of theatre production would change my life. In 1994 I started a drama group. The students named it Encore Young People's Stage Company.*

Every year, forty young people ranging in age from six to nineteen join together to form Encore. Our group gives each member a creative voice that is respected and encouraged. We have an informal board of directors that votes on all major financial decisions and appropriates funds for each production.

During the school year, Encore meets twice a month for classes in body movement, voice techniques, and production skills. The classes help prepare the students for the year-end production, which we perform for area schools and the general public.

We have learned a lot together. The students have acquired acting skills, stage presence, and production know-how. Most importantly, we have created a community. Children and their parents have invested themselves in the project and in one another, creating a close-knit group.

The students do all of the acting and most of the production work. The Encore students are knowledgeable about William

* Encore Young People's Stage Company is an informal drama group in Wolfeboro, New Hampshire, not to be confused with the nonprofit Encore Theater Company in Kingston, New Hampshire.

Shakespeare and have performed a number of his plays. I affectionately call us a cult of Shakespearean Nerds living deep in the
heart of New England. We have chosen Shakespeare's plays for
several reasons:

- They are public domain (no royalty fees).
- They are classics, which serves the students well through-
  out their academic careers and lives.
- Shakespeare is adaptable to various historical periods.
  We have created stage direction, narration, and music to
  accompany them. (For more on stage adaptations, see
  Resources section.)

The Encore students love Shakespeare and often quote him,
finding his words to be inspirational, funny, or simply to the
point. I often hear, "Scurvy knave, put up thy weapon" or, " I can
live no longer by thinking" or, one of their favorites, "All the
world's a stage." During our production of *Much Ado About
Nothing*, the students presented me with a T-shirt imprinted on
the front with the words "All the world's a stage . . . the rest is
just Much Ado About Nothing."

The steps involved with starting a community theatre
group for young people are outlined in this book. I hope you
find it helpful, encouraging, and educational. The only limita-
tion you may bump up against is untapped imagination. Give
the students the opportunity to explore their creativity, and
stand back. They will fly with it!

"Bid your friends welcome, and show a merry cheer."
—*Merchant of Venice*

# ...■1■ Building a Strong Foundation

## The Process and the Goal

The main goal of Encore Young People's Stage Company is to give every member a chance to be onstage. The transformation young people experience while working in the performing arts is a continual revelation for me, and something I did not anticipate when I began the work.

Relationships are at the heart of theatre work. At best, the group dynamic can be complex, multilayered, rich, and rewarding. At worst, it can be degrading, false, and demoralizing. It is important to create and maintain a safe atmosphere through mutual respect.

Young people can be perceptive when given the chance. Listening is crucial. I try to remind myself often to open my ears more than my mouth. An adult who listens attentively helps create an atmosphere of respect for each person's ideas.

The sense of accomplishment that results from a successful theatre production endows students with self-confidence and consideration for others. Give young people authentic work in the real world, with high levels of responsibility, and they will rise to the occasion. The Encore students have consistently surpassed my expectations. When young people are focused and given strong direction, they will be less likely to find their "kicks" in drugs, alcohol, and unhealthy relationships.

By its nature, theatre is an act of giving. I know the Encore students have richly blessed our small community with quality theatre productions of Shakespearean plays. Stage work is an opportunity for actors and production crew to give of themselves in ways many of them never before experienced. When

1

fourteen-year-old Jen started the program, she was too self-conscious to approach anyone she didn't know well. By the end of the first year she had come out of her shell, and her generosity of spirit has been a great asset to the entire group.

My goals are simple:

1. Give young people authentic work in the theatre.
2. Value each voice individually.
3. Set high standards.

Your goals may be different, but keep in mind that stage work is about process.

## Setting Boundaries and Clarifying Expectations

Opening the doors to a theatrical production does not require prior experience, but it hinges on good organization. Here are some suggestions for setting boundaries and communicating your expectations.

*Make everything clear.* We have various rules that we consider to be important for the group. Make sure everyone knows the rules starting the first day. You may need to repeat the rules at the beginning of each session so that there are no misunderstandings.

*Set rules for the use of the building.* Inside the theatre we discuss the importance of valuing public property. We have rules concerning the various places in a building we are allowed to use, and a parent organizes small groups of students to keep these areas clean. This works well because we know who is responsible for what.

*Set rules about behavior.* At the beginning, remind the students of the standard of behavior to which your theatre group aspires. Encourage them to:

- Reach out to one another.
- Support one another.
- Respect each person's creative ideas. (Do not tolerate ridicule in any form.)
- Be attentive when someone is onstage.

*Create a safe environment.* We do a lot of experimentation with acting techniques, so it is essential that we build a safe environment where the students feel free from ridicule and failure and secure in exploring ideas.

- Be supportive as students discover and create.
- Be clear and consistent about the rules.
- Encourage students to invest in the project by making it their own.
- Treat everyone with equal importance and respect.
- Stress teamwork as a source of strength.
- Build a sense of belonging to the group. (This can be extended to the larger community.)
- Remind students that there is no failure in art.

"I do now let loose."

# ▪ ▪ ▪ 2 ▪ Warm-Ups

Warming up before doing theatre work—whether a workshop or going onstage for a performance—helps the students to loosen up mentally and physically. Keep it light, fun, and loose.

## Stretching and Balancing Exercises

Gather everyone into a circle. Start with stretching both arms up as high as you can. I always say, "Reach for the stars," because that's what I encourage them to do creatively.

Then lean forward and drop both hands down toward the ground and stretch. Don't let anyone hurt themselves. Remind them to push only until they feel a good stretch and then back off. This is not a competition to see who can stretch the farthest.

Next concentrate on the neck muscles by doing gentle rotations. Stress being *gentle*—our necks are fragile parts of our anatomy and can easily be injured by overdoing any of the stretches.

Rotate the shoulders after the neck exercises. Do both shoulders together, forward and back twice, and then do each shoulder separately. This is a great way to relieve tension that builds in the upper body. Remind the students to do this right before they go onstage to help use up their nervous energy and relieve mounting tension.

Bend side to side with nice long stretches, arms extended to loosen the muscles along the sides of the torso. Think of stretching every part of the body, starting with the head and working down to the toes, stretching each area.

Next do some balancing exercises. Balancing is an important way to bring the energy of the group into focus. Have the students carefully concentrate on a spot on the floor and hold up their right leg with their right hand. Once balanced, stretch out the leg being held up, and hold. Repeat the stretch with the left leg.

Finish by clasping both hands behind the waist and bending forward while raising the arms skyward. This is an excellent exercise for stretching the chest muscles and opening up the lungs.

After all the stretching, shake your arms and legs and then the whole body. This usually gets everyone laughing. The stretching and balancing exercises only take about ten minutes but they are essential to warming up the body for stage work.

## Voice Warm-Up

Voice development is crucial to acting. We do a lot of voice training and, right from the start, I try to help young people learn to project their voices. Projecting takes a while to understand and master. It's what I call "finding a person's real voice." Our voices are powerful instruments of communication. Learning how to control them is a lifetime skill.

Warm up the voice by enunciating the vowels using the face muscles, opening the mouth as wide as possible and stretching out each sound for several seconds: *A, E, I, O, U.* Then work on some consonants: *bah, bah, bah, th, th, th, dee, dee, dee,* et cetera.

This exercise helps build awareness of how we enunciate words. End the voice warm-up by taking a deep inhalation and saying *Ahhhhhh* until you run out of breath.

## Group Work

After warming up our bodies and our voices, it's important to get the students to warm up to each other. The following exercises create positive energy and strengthen the group dynamic.

### HANDSHAKE

Ask the students to make two separate lines facing one another. Have them shake the hand of the person across from them while saying something nice. Then repeat the process three or four times with different partners. Usually this gets a group feeling good about being together.

### Circle Walk

During the circle walk, everyone walks in a large circle while I call out different scenarios. For example, I might say, "Walk like you have just won the lottery" or, "Walk like you have just come out of a three-hour meeting." The students love this exercise and always ask for it. Do the activity for five to ten minutes, depending on group size.

### Mirror Work

Mirror work is fun, once the group members feel comfortable with one another.

Have each student pick a partner, and have each pair of partners stand facing each other. Designate one person as the "mirror," who reflects, movement for movement, what the other person is doing. This takes intense concentration while looking into each other's eyes. I have seen some phenomenal work between students as they do a beautiful slow dancelike mime.

Mirror work is not something to ask a new group to do together, because it can really intimidate young people when they are just getting to know one another. Once you feel the group is established and comfortable together, however, mirror work can be a powerful exercise.

### The Lean

Another activity I like to use with the group is called the lean. Everyone takes a partner and the two begin by leaning against each other back-to-back. The pairs slowly crouch down into a squat on the floor and then come back up to a standing position. Then, leaning shoulder-to-shoulder, each pair slowly walks around the room.

Sometimes four students will get together and figure out a way to lean against one another and move in the same direction. This teaches them about trust, which is essential to stage work.

"Knowledge is the wing where with we fly to heaven."

# ∎ ∎ ∎ 3 ∎ Acting Techniques

## Body Movement

Body language is universal; it is the wise actor who studies it through careful observation. Encourage students to watch people, to notice their movements, how they gesture, the way they walk, and how they stand.

Practice and experiment with a variety of body movements and dance. Generally speaking, the six-to-ten-year-olds are free and easy with their bodies. At this age they are not self-conscious and are eager to try all sorts of creative movements. The eleven-to-fifteen-year-olds are the toughest. That is the time in a young person's life when so much energy goes into "being cool." They are extremely self-conscious and are terrified of making a mistake and looking foolish. The sixteen-to-nineteen-year-olds are a mixed bag. Some are graceful and move with ease and power, and some are still getting used to their taller, larger bodies and feel awkward. But this age group is more open to seeing what is possible.

Again, creating a safe environment is absolutely necessary. Holding up a high standard of respect and consideration for others is vital.

Below are some activities for creative movement.

### MASK WORK

This is a fantastic way of getting the group to loosen up. Hiding behind a mask can give even the most self-conscious students courage to play and experiment with body movement. It works great for new groups as well as for more seasoned ones. (If you do not have masks, see the section on mask making in Chapter 7 for instructions on how to make your own.)

During class, ask the students to put on a mask, get onstage, and move. Play music or give them a skit to perform, or let them create their own dance or mime.

9

Using masks in performance as disguises or special effects can add to the power of a scene. Characters can take on different personae, which creates stunning effects onstage.

**Mask-Work Ideas**

- Create simple masks using poster board, paper bags, paper plates, and Magic Markers. Attach to the face with elastic, or glue the mask to a stick so that it can be held in front of the face.
- Give students an idea of what you want onstage by putting a mask on yourself and moving across the stage in a dramatic fashion.
- Let them try different masks and experiment with body movement in front of a large mirror.
- Play music, and let them loosen up through dance while wearing their masks.

## PANTOMIME

Focus on body movement through pantomime. Give the students a scenario (see ideas below) and remind them that a good skit is like a good story—it has a beginning, a middle, and an end, and a conflict that gets resolved. Allow about five or ten minutes for the students to create something, and then have them perform it. Most of the time the skits will be humorous.

A skit without words is especially fun to watch. Everyone moves with exaggerated gestures to try to get the audience to understand the action of the scene. This also gives the students an opportunity to see what works and what doesn't onstage. Pantomimes help students to develop an eye for stage movement as they watch their friends perform various skits.

**Pantomime Ideas**

1. A dance troop is performing when one member breaks his or her toe.
2. A family is locked out of their house.
3. People are driving in a car that has a flat tire.

4. Someone visits a nursing home and all the residents fall asleep.

5. The air-conditioning comes on in a restaurant and the patrons slowly freeze.

6. A group of people who are allergic to cats visit a house full of cats.

You get the idea. To start, keep the ideas light and funny.

### LIVE MARIONETTES

This is an activity that requires pairing up. One person acts as a puppeteer and the other as a marionette. The puppeteer stands onstage and the marionette is positioned on the floor below the stage. Give the students a few minutes to work up a short skit. Many times the students will want to collaborate in performing a puppet show together. Make sure you emphasize that the puppeteer can also make some very creative moves.

**Marionette Ideas**

- Have four or five pairs work together on a scene or skit in which the marionettes interact.
- Have the marionette trade places with the puppeteer as part of the skit.
- Have the marionettes, in an onstage transformation, turn into humans.

### ADD A PEARL

Students have choreographed some great dances through this activity, and it gives everyone a chance to see his or her own creative ideas come to life.

Break everyone into groups of five to eight people. Have each individual take a turn and create some kind of body movement. Then string all the ideas together into a dance, with each student memorizing all the movements. The resulting dance can be performed in a line, a circle, or rows; anything goes.

This is effective not only for learning body movement but also for strengthening the memory. Once you get to actually preparing a play, there is a tremendous amount of memorization work required. The more you incorporate activities to help develop memorization skills, the more confidence the group will have onstage.

### Add-a-Pearl Ideas

Have them create their movements with a theme in mind, such as

- dancing in the rain
- a celebratory dance
- a formal dance
- a slow dance
- a dance for a solemn occasion

### IN THE MANNER OF THE WORD

This is a fun game that works best for groups of ten or twelve.

Each group chooses someone to go out of the room. (He or she becomes the "outsider.") The group then decides on a word that describes a motion (an adverb) that ends in "ly." Examples: *happily, angrily, foolishly, clumsily,* et cetera. Any word that describes an action will do. After the group decides on a word, the outsider reenters.

Now the fun begins. The outsider has to try to guess what the word is by asking different individuals to do things "in the manner of the word." For example, the outsider can ask an individual to go across the room and open the door "in the manner of the word." The chosen individual must then perform the action in a way that the outsider can guess what the word is. When the outsider correctly guesses, then the person who was acting out the word becomes the outsider and the group selects a new word. This is a popular activity among all ages.

### In-the-Manner-of-the-Word Ideas

1. Start with fairly simple words and work up to more difficult adverbs that take some creative thinking to act out.

2. For a real challenge, try words such as *ambivalently, spiritually,* and *doggedly,* which can make for some hilarious pantomimes.

## *Voice Training*

Training students to speak clearly and enunciate their words gives them a skill that will serve them well throughout their lives. Becoming aware of the quality of our voices is enlightening. Some people have beautiful speaking voices; it is like listening to music when they talk. But most of us go around totally unaware of the power of vocal expression.

In theatre work, the voice is vitally important. Without learning to project and control it, the actor's time onstage is ineffectual and boring.

Any time we are actively doing voice exercises on a daily basis, the quality of our speaking changes. The quality of our singing is dramatically improved also. Young people's voices go through many changes, boys' especially. If students are exposed to voice training when they are young, they will become aware of the power of speech and learn to communicate more effectively.

I have worked with many teens who mumble, or speak so quickly they are impossible to understand. Through voice training they learn to speak clearly and project their voices beautifully while onstage. While I wish I could report that they always go on to speak clearly offstage, they don't. However, I am thrilled when they come to a place of knowing how to enunciate their words and project their voices, being able to create a more powerful presence onstage. And maybe someday they will tap into what they learned about vocal expression and perceive its value in everyday life.

### VOICE PROJECTION

Voice projection depends entirely on breath control. Start by doing deep diaphragmatic breathing: nice long inhalations and exhaling while saying *Ahhhhh.*

To illustrate where the diaphragm is, instruct each student to place his or her hand over the muscles right below the rib cage. Inhale deeply. Ask them what happens to their muscles. (You will get varying answers.)

Now tell the students to lie flat on their backs and place one hand on their chest and the other on their diaphragm. Take a deep inhalation and feel the chest rise, then make the muscles of the diaphragm also expand. You should feel both your hands move up and down with each breath. Taking a diaphragmatic breath means breathing all the way into the diaphragm. Projecting the voice entails pushing the voice out with the power of a diaphragmatic breath. It takes a while to find the right place, but with experience it comes.

It may be awkward at first but with some practice you will feel your chest expand and you will be able to breathe more deeply. (Tell the students that if they begin to feel dizzy, they should stop.)

Being relaxed and breathing deeply will give everyone's voice more volume without the actors having to yell. Many children think that projecting their voices means screaming their lines out so the audience can hear them. Unfortunately, as children raise their voices they begin to squeak. The result is language that is impossible to understand and unbearable to listen to. Even young children can expand their lungs through breathing exercises and learn to project their voices well.

During the breathing exercises help them experiment with the sounds produced by their vocal chords. Take a deep breath and exhale while making various sounds like *zzzzzz*, or *grrrrrrrrrr*, or *shhhh*.

Enunciation is essential in projecting the voice. Encourage the students to practice breathing exercises, making various sounds, and tongue twisters (see below) at home. Even two weeks of daily practice will result in more volume and clearer speech.

Always take the time to warm up the voice. Vocal chords can be damaged if projection is undertaken without warming the voice up first. If there are performers who are losing their voices from trying to project, give them a day or two to rest before trying again. Teach your students to be as careful of their voices as they would be with a valuable musical instrument.

## Enunciation Work

Since we perform Shakespeare, it is crucial that the actors enunciate their lines clearly, and since most of our audiences have had little exposure to Shakespeare, the success of the play depends on how clearly the actors can express themselves verbally.

Having the group recite tongue twisters aloud is an excellent exercise. An example of a tongue twister is "Rubber baby-buggy bumpers." When reciting tongue twisters, overenunciate each word, speaking slowly and clearly. This seems like an ineffectual exercise, but for many young people it is the first time they have been exposed to the concept and practice of slowly articulating their words.

Generally, Americans do not speak clearly. We talk quickly and slur many of our words together. We especially drop the last few letters of many words as we sail through sentences trying to express ourselves as quickly as possible. This is the conversational standard to which our children are accustomed, so it is naturally the way they express themselves verbally.

Slowing down is new territory for many students. Find some tongue twisters in a book or ask the students to contribute some. Enunciate each tongue twister carefully and slowly to the group. Let them hear it spoken correctly. Resist the temptation to speed up while reciting the tongue twister, as that will defeat the purpose.

I tell students to feel how the different words make the tongue and mouth move. I also point out that Shakespeare was a poet, and that the sounds of his words are as important as their meaning. Poets have spent time thinking of how words feel in our mouths. Each word is carefully chosen for meaning as well as music.

### Enunciation Exercises

1. Recite tongue twisters.
2. Overenunciate each word.
3. Have students listen and note differences in the ways people speak.

### LINE BY LINE

In theatre work, the passages of dialogue that the actors speak are called lines. This exercise helps us realize that how we say our lines changes the meaning of what we are saying. Example: the line "Yes, come in, the door is open," could be said in a friendly voice, or with impatience, or very businesslike. Often the students can make some very subtle changes in their voices and completely change the meaning of the line.

### Line-by-Line Exercise

1. Write different one-line sentences on strips of paper.
2. Place them in a hat or bowl.
3. Ask each student to pick a line, go onstage, and read it aloud three different ways.

## METRONOME WORK

Many teens speak so fast, it is hard to understand them. It is a natural inclination to speak quickly onstage because of nervousness. If we are aware of this situation, we can help the actors slow down their lines before dealing with the excitement and nervousness of going onstage in front of an audience.

Here is an idea, conceived by one of our musicians, to help us slow down. The exercise works best with individuals and requires a metronome.

Have the student say her lines aloud. Set the metronome to the speed she is talking. It is usually set at a pretty fast clip. Then slow down the metronome and have the student slow down her lines to that level. This helps the student get the idea of how fast-paced his or her speech is. If you slow it way down, then the student can also work on enunciation.

If you are working with Shakespeare, you will find that clapping out rhythms with your hands is immensely helpful, because Shakespearean plays are written in poetry, with the meter being iambic (a metrical foot of two syllables with the first syllable unaccented and the second accented, like the beating of the human heart, de *dum* de *dum*) pentameter (a line of verse, containing five metrical feet). The use of a metronome, or the clapping of hands, as a tool for the student to hear the beat of the poetry, is illuminating.

### Metronome Exercise

1. Time a metronome to the natural way the actor delivers his or her lines.
2. Slow the metronome down and have the actor read the lines slower and slower to the beat of the metronome.

## SINGING

If you have musicians in your group, get them involved. I have slowly introduced singing into our theatre group. At first the students were tentative about it, but as we have gone along they have enjoyed singing and are finding their musical voices.

Singing is something that most of us want to try whether or not we think we can. It is usually in our childhoods that an insensitive remark from an adult crushes our desire to ever sing again. As author Robert Fulghum notes in his book *Uh-Oh*, a vast difference between kindergarten and college-age students is the willingness to spontaneously sing a song, dance, or paint a picture. It is unfortunate that we are so often taught that if we can't do something at a professional level, we shouldn't do it at all. A supportive, playful environment in community theatre can help us all rekindle the sheer fun of singing.

I used to think that anyone could sing, but through the years I have worked with a few adults and children who were truly tone deaf. Even though these same people may play instruments beautifully, their ears are not tuned to being able to sing. However, I feel that with enough work and a good voice teacher, most anyone can sing. Think of Rex Harrison as Professor Higgins in *My Fair Lady*. Singing is a powerful and soulful expression. It can bring a scene alive in a play. Having an able chorus is an asset to any theatre group. I highly recommend a tape series called *Born to Sing* (see Resources section). The tapes give voice exercises and enough information about singing to get started with a group of students. Ask around and perhaps you'll find a singer in your group willing to help.

"Frame your mind to mirth and merriment."

## Improvisation

Improvisation is defined in the theatre world as a spontaneous creative process in which actors perform with little or no preparation. It is a great technique to learn, as it enables actors to think quickly in front of an audience.

We do a lot of "improv" work. The Encore students love the spontaneity of it. As you work with improvisation, your students will grow in self-confidence. Learning improvisational techniques helps develop an attitude of grace during difficult situations in real life.

Recently, during the filming of a dress rehearsal for *Twelfth Night*, a couple of the Encore actors fumbled their lines and, without batting an eye, one of the actresses stepped forward and saved the scene by improvising until they were all back on track. I was genuinely impressed. Imagine having to ad-lib in Elizabethan! Sometimes young people have no clue as to how talented they are.

Following are some effective exercises for practicing improvisation.

## Skits

Skits are exciting and fun ways to help the actors get to know one another. When doing skits as an exercise:

1. Break into small groups of about seven or eight students.
2. Put each group in different areas of the room.
3. Offer each group an idea for a skit (see below) and give them about five or ten minutes to put it together.
4. Have each group perform their skit.

While they are practicing their skits, walk around the room and make sure that all the students are working together. Remind them that a good scene has a beginning, a middle, and an end, and that there is a problem or conflict to resolve.

**Skit Ideas**

1. Old people in a room who can't hear the TV.
2. People riding in a bus that gets lost.
3. Children visit the zoo.
4. Mad scientists conduct an experiment.
5. Construction workers become confused about what they are building.
6. Various people, such as a homeless old man and a rich old woman, a child and a monkey, interact at a park.
7. Someone attempts to talk a group of people watching skydiving into trying it themselves.
8. A woman tries to talk on the telephone while her children act up.

Get the idea? Anything goes! Start with light ideas that can be developed into something funny.

If you want to use skits as a way of teaching older teens about the tough situations in life, this is also a great tool. Make sure the group is close and feeling secure before trying anything that may get too dramatic.

Teens are capable of showing intense feelings onstage. However, they need to feel confident that it is safe to do so, and that no one will laugh at them in ridicule. Again, it is up to the director to set the tone; hold up a high standard of behavior and praise their efforts. The rest of the group will follow. If you are in the situation of students making fun of each other, nip it in the bud. For theatre work to be successful it is essential that students show respect for one another.

### PROPS IN A BAG

Ahead of time, prepare four or five bags with different props in each. A prop is defined as any object used in performance onstage. In each bag place five to ten objects: shoelaces, old newspapers, hats, pencils, an old shoe, and so on.

Divide students into small groups of about five or six and hand each group a bag. Each group must come up with a skit using all the props in the bag. Give them ten minutes to work up a skit, then get out of the way and watch the ideas fly.

#### Props-in-a-Bag Exercise

1. Put a small number of objects in a bag.
2. Divide the students into small groups.
3. Give each group a bag of objects and about ten minutes to work out a skit using the objects in the bag.

### ADD A CHARACTER

When you have ten or fifteen minutes left in a class, this is a good spur-of-the-moment improvisational exercise that can be brought to an end at any time.

Have everyone sit in a large circle, and ask five or six students to go into the center. Give the students a quick scenario, such as painting a house. As they improvise the scene, students sitting in the circle may go into the center and join the action, adding a new character. Every time a new actor joins the action, one who is already there needs to go out.

It is fun to step in and entirely change the scene. For example, if four or five students are improvising the painting of a house, someone can enter the scene and change it by yelling, "There's a fire down the street. Come see!" A few moments later, another student may join in and change it again. This kind of exercise is great for freeing the imagination.

### Add-a-Character Exercise

1. Students sit in a large circle.
2. Five or six students begin improvising a skit in the middle of the circle.
3. Other students join in to add to or change the action, and each time a new actor enters, one who is already there exits the scene.

Improvisation is a lifetime skill. No matter what careers your students may aspire to, improvisational skills will serve them well.

## BUILD A CHARACTER

Creating a believable character takes time and it can be a difficult job, requiring insight, sensitivity, and intelligence. The ability to create a believable role can be developed by observing people closely. Ask your students to describe how personality traits are manifested through body language and voice quality.

During play rehearsals, make time for open discussions about the different roles in the play that you are performing. I make myself available to the actors, in small groups as well as individually, during the course of a production. This is essential to strong acting and gives each of the students the opportunity to analyze the play in depth.

### Tips for Building a Character

1. Let students find their stage character through discussion and analysis.
2. Invite their ideas of how their characters would react to the action of the play.
3. Give them time to experiment during rehearsals.
4. Let them run through a scene many times so that they can fully understand the action as well as the motivation of each character.

During our rehearsals for *Romeo and Juliet*, the young man who played the role of the priest did a lot of work on character analysis. When he first started, he wanted to play the role like it was played in the popular movie starring Leonardo DiCaprio. I wanted something with greater depth. After reading the script a number of times and talking about what motivated the priest, the student played the role with such care and understanding that he often brought tears to my eyes. I always try to remind myself to be open to each student's perceptions so that I can learn from each of them.

## Working Together: Cooperative Activities

The success of all theatre work depends on the collaboration of many creative individuals. There are no solo stars in young people's stage work. A successful theatre group learns to work well together, honoring each member for the unique qualities he or she brings to the group.

Here are some ideas that will help foster a collaborative spirit for everyone involved.

### LARGE-CIRCLE SIT-DOWN

This requires a large group (at least twenty people), concentration, and an element of trust between individuals. Have the group form a circle with everyone facing the same way (each student facing the back of the student in front). Ask the students to stand close together. Then, at the same time, have them slowly sit down. Each person sits on the knees of the person behind him, so that each person has someone on his or her lap.

If you do this slowly it will work. However, if it's done too fast someone usually topples over, and then everyone goes down . . . amid great laughter. We have accomplished this with up to sixty-five people and we were all able to sit down together and hold the position long enough to enjoy the sensation. When it's time to get up, everyone needs to do so at exactly the same moment. This activity builds the feeling of being able to depend on each other, while having fun in the process.

Word of caution: Be sure that very small students are not right behind or in front of very large ones, or someone could get hurt.

### Large-Circle Sit-Down Exercise

1. Get everyone into a circle.
2. Have everyone face the back of the student in front.
3. Slowly sit down on one another's laps and hold this position.
4. Stand up straight again as a group.

## BUILD A MACHINE

This exercise is particularly effective to help a group loosen up because it's easy and no one has to say a word.

Choose a student to go onstage and do a simple mechanical action, such as bending forward and moving his or her arms in an up-and-down motion while making the sound of a machine. Ask another student to join in with a new action and sound, connecting himself with the first. Keep building the machine with new students until everyone is connected to one another. You might choose to play music and have the students move to the beat.

### Build-a-Machine Exercise

1. Choose one student to create a specific type of mechanical motion—for instance, a clock mechanism—while making an appropriate noise.
2. Have others join in, doing their own motion and sound.

## RESOLVE THE CONFLICT

Learning to solve problems is a skill that requires sensitivity and practice. Theatre work provides excellent opportunities to work on conflict-resolution strategies that can open avenues of communication between students.

In the context of a skit, give the group a problem or a conflict and let them solve it onstage. For example, give them a scenario that requires diplomacy, such as a Democratic president coming to see a play directed by a very outspoken Republican. This kind of problem solving, which requires quick thinking, gives students an opportunity to consider how to deal with different types of people and situations, and how to be sensitive to the feelings of those involved. Of course, depending on the age of the students, the conflicts can be handled in a lighthearted way or used to open up more serious discussions.

When we do problem-solving skits, I don't give the students any time to rehearse. The actors get onstage and do the scene without communicating with their fellow players beforehand. Learning to improvise is a skill that can be greatly improved through practice. Real life provides infinite ideas for scenarios to improvise on stage. The possibilities are endless.

### Resolve-the-Conflict Skit Ideas

1. Many people want the same role in a play.
2. Last-minute scheduling changes disrupt a festival.
3. It is discovered that someone has lied.
4. A large misunderstanding gets published on the front page of the local newspaper.
5. A student loses something valuable of her parents that she didn't have permission to use.

## Putting It All Together

Body, mind, heart, and soul go into acting. Theatre provides a unique opportunity to develop every aspect of ourselves. The first step is becoming aware of the way we move, how we speak, the words we choose, and the way we think. In a growing child, theatre work can be an avenue for exploring communication techniques and self-expression. Success onstage can have lasting effects on a young person's development.

Putting it all together is the next step in the process of working toward a production. After practicing the body movement, voice training, and improvisational techniques, the group will be ready to begin preparing for an actual production. Still, there's a great deal to learn and a lot of work ahead . . . and much more fun than you could ever imagine!

This is the point where your group-as-a-community will develop and grow, giving each person a chance to shine and get in touch with his or her own genius. So go for it, and take joy in the process, knowing that in order to grow we must stretch. There are valuable lessons to learn and skills to develop. All the activities up to this point have been laying the foundation for a performance of which everyone can be proud.

"Let me be your servant." —*Twelfth Night*

# ■ ■ ■ 4 ■ The Play

## *Choosing the Play*

I'll be honest; I have an agenda whenever I choose a play. My agenda is this: I want a play that's educational, complex, and enlightening, with a plot that younger students can follow, and characters that have enough substance to give the older students something to chew on. I want the setting of the play to have enough history to make it interesting. I also want there to be plenty of characters, some big-group scenes, some humorous scenes, and a place where I can add a large dance number. Sounds like a lot to look for, but every year we have found the perfect play.

You are going to spend a lot of time on a play, hearing the lines over and over and over again. It had better be something you love, or you will tire of it before the first performance. That's why I have always done Shakespeare. It thrills me to hear students reciting the lines of a Shakespearean play. It is an educational opportunity for us to engage in the work of the Bard. Shakespeare is so beautiful; his poetry has the power to engross and enlighten audiences and performers alike.

When choosing a play, remember: If it is a contemporary play, you will need to pay royalties as well as purchase the scripts. Be careful not to break any copyright laws, which protect artists and their work. Honor the creative integrity of playwrights and make sure you have permission to perform the play you choose. (See the Resources section for a list of catalogs that sell play scripts.)

When choosing a play, consider the following three questions.

1. Does the play have substance? Or is it just something silly written for children?
2. Is it truthful; is justice served in the end?
3. Does it fit your group, and if not, can you make it fit?

Making a play "fit" has always been a source of great joy and an enormous amount of work for me. Because Shakespeare is public domain, I edit his plays so that they are between 90 and 120 minutes in length. I have also turned some of the male characters into female parts, and I write in a narrator or two to help explain the story. I do not change any of the original language, but I do shorten some of the soliloquies and remove some of the more obscure passages. It takes me from eighty to a hundred hours to do this. It's a labor of love on my part, but do not be daunted. In the Resources section of this book are edited versions of Shakespeare's plays, as well as information on how you can purchase some of the scripts I have adapted.

One of the most important jobs for the director is choosing a good play, one that is a good fit for your group. Once you have done that, you can fully engage in the process of producing a masterpiece.

## Auditions

The first step after deciding on a play is to bring it to the group and introduce it to them. Explain the story, the action, and the main characters, so that the students know what the play is about before they try out for a role. This is an important step; it gives them time to think about the roles they want and it gets them invested in the project. Give each of them a script so that they can rehearse a scene to perform during tryouts. Schedule audition times.

I have tried various ways of holding auditions. Auditioning is a diffcult time for the students, as most get nervous, so try to loosen them up before doing the actual readings. The warm-up exercises in Chapter 2 are a good way to shake off some of their nervous energy.

Before auditions, I go through the play and find some scenes that show a range of emotions but not so much action. I make sure everyone has a good chance at reading a part. Keep in mind that some students do not read aloud well but are capable of great work onstage.

It's important to explain how professionals cast a play. A professional director explained to me that he tries to find actors who are as close as possible to the part he is casting. He looks for actors who are comfortable being themselves and who show authenticity during their audition.

Tell the group that casting a play is like fitting the pieces of a puzzle together. Oftentimes it's important to look the part. Not everyone can have a leading role but everyone will have a part. What they do with the part is up to them. Point out that Judi Dench's Oscar-winning performance in *Shakespeare in Love* was only eight and a half minutes in length. What she created in that short amount of time was an unforgettable Queen Elizabeth of enormous power and complexity.

It's crucial to encourage the students to do their best. Equally important is to make sure that everyone is quiet when others are auditioning. Respect and encouragement are two elements to keep in mind throughout the entire production process.

## Casting

When I first started directing plays, I did the casting alone. It was the only thing about the process that I dreaded. The great difficulty in casting a play with young people is that their hearts are set on playing a certain character and they can't always have the roles they want.

Now I have help with casting from the board of directors for Encore. There is a group of us who struggle together through the process, so that no individual bears the burden of disappointing a student not chosen for a coveted role.

You want to be fair. You want the production to be good. You want the students to fit the roles as much as possible. And you want to make everyone happy. Unfortunately, you can't always accomplish this last item. To make sure everyone who wants to be onstage will be, include a number of crowd scenes. The dance numbers are another opportunity for solos and small-group actions that spotlight actors who have minor parts. I also try to fill in scenes with "extras" whenever I can. By the end of the performance, usually all the students feel that they have had a good-sized part. The trick is to showcase everyone and spotlight their unique talents.

## Scheduling

Scheduling a production is a very important task. Take time to think this through. Being organized is the key to success. Once you have the script and cast, your next step is the critical organizational work of scheduling rehearsal time and production time.

### REHEARSALS

First, break all scenes down into three categories.

1. The long scenes
2. The middle-sized scenes
3. The shorter scenes

Schedule two separate times for each scene, one to block the scene, the other to go over the blocking. (Blocking is explained below.)

Second, schedule two long rehearsal times. During the first rehearsal, string the first half of the play together. Use the second rehearsal to pull together the second half of the play. Depending on the length of the production, allow at least two hours for each of these rehearsals.

Third, schedule four or five rehearsal times during the week before opening night. Remember to schedule a technical rehearsal. Use the time for the light crew, stage manager, and crew to rehearse their light cues and scene changes. This is the week all of us love most. It is exciting and full of action. On the first day (usually a long Sunday afternoon) we do one complete run-through, take a break, and then have a dress rehearsal. This gives the costume committee time to make alterations the following day. It is important to recognize that the production crew may need to make construction changes to the set during the week before opening night. We do two or three dress rehearsals before the first performance.

Scheduling rehearsal times is not as difficult as it may seem. You will want to give yourself enough time to do the play, but not so much time that you lose momentum.

Allow extra time for:

- long crowd scenes
- dance scenes
- scenes of great emotional intensity

Just think about what happens during each scene and plan accordingly.

Early rehearsals mainly involve blocking the scenes. Ask the actors to have all their lines memorized by a certain date. Rehearsing action scenes is impossible when students have a script in their hands.

After scheduling all the scenes, the next step is to make a calendar of scene rehearsals, and list the characters needed for each rehearsal time. Make copies and be sure that each student's parents have a schedule.

## PRODUCTIONS

After scheduling rehearsal times, schedule production times. Set a time when the set committee can build the set and the light technicians can set up the lights; preferably not at the same time. The light technicians need to have the stage and auditorium all to themselves for a number of hours. If you don't give them this time, frustration between the crew will ensue. The lights can be quite complicated, so make sure that you schedule plenty of time to do the work.

Remember that you have four very different activities happening in the theatre during the course of a production:

1. Rehearsals
2. Set construction
3. Lights
4. Costume designing and sewing

I will go into these in more detail later, but remember: you need stage time for the first three. Make sure you schedule enough time for each activity. Depending on the production, your lighting crew will need anywhere from four to fifteen hours for a small- to medium-sized production.

## Blocking Scenes

Blocking means to place the actors where you want them to be onstage during a scene. Here are a few things to be aware of when blocking each scene.

First, make sure that, from the audience, all the actors can be seen and that the actors face toward the audience when they are speaking. Young actors tend to want to turn toward each other when they are conversing, but unless they face toward the audience, the actors cannot be heard.

Second, where there is more dialogue than action, block scenes by making the actors move in interesting ways. Consider different floor heights on stage so that the actors can step up or sit down. Once you are sitting in the front row of the theatre you can automatically see what works and what doesn't.

Third, always go to rehearsals prepared and organized. Read through the scenes ahead of time and have a good idea of what you want before you get to the theatre. Remember to give your actors freedom to experiment. Being a good director means being able to think quickly on your feet. Give each actor respect for his or her creative ideas. Use everything you can without compromising the integrity of the show.

When I see an action that doesn't work, I'll say something like, "I love what you're doing in the first part of this scene but for some reason the middle part isn't working. Lets try another idea. What else do you think would work?" This way I am praising what I like about a student's performance before I ask for something different. The student is usually eager to try another approach and often gets it right on the mark the next time through.

Blocking is a visual process. All the scenes need to be dynamic and interesting to watch. Make sure that even the shortest scenes can capture and hold the audience's attention.

## Learning Lines

Memorizing lines is more difficult for some students than for others. It is great to develop memorization skills, which enhance our learning ability. Even when we are not in production I encourage the students to learn poetry. The more we use the part of our brain that enables us to memorize, the more developed it becomes.

It is essential to memorize the lines as soon as possible so that the actors' hands are free from holding the script. An effective technique for memorizing lines is audiotaping the entire play, then making copies for each actor. The students have informed me that this is a tremendous help.

I schedule a deadline for learning lines. The assistant director is always by my side during rehearsals and reads along in the script, prompting the actors as necessary. This saves me from having to read along while trying to watch the action onstage.

All lines must be learned at home; rehearsal time is for blocking and practicing with the other players. With a lot of encouragement, the students will learn their lines. If it's obvious that a student is really struggling with the memorization, be extra patient and help him or her to break down the task into manageable pieces. Work out a schedule of deadlines and write it down on a calendar for the student.

Included on the following page is a list of helpful hints that can be photocopied and passed around to the students to assist them in learning their lines.

## Building a Cooperative Cast

Theatre is a learning process, and much of its success hinges on the relationships among the production's participants. Making sure that the cast and crew get along well and have a good time goes hand in hand with the hard work and focus it takes to put on a great show. In order to build a strong group, individuals need to invest in one another. To encourage this, I give short pep talks at each rehearsal. I tell the cast how important it is to give to one another, to take care of one another, and to make sure that everything is going smoothly.

**Helpful Hints for Learning Your Lines**

1. Make sure that you understand all the words and the meaning of what you are saying.

2. Watch for word patterns. The way words are grouped by punctuation tells us how they are to be spoken.

   When you see a        : colon

                         ? question mark

                         . period    You come to a full stop in your speech.

   When you see a        ; semicolon

                         , comma

                         — dash    You pause in your speech.

3. Think of the importance of sound and silence in your lines. Also notice the effects of short abrupt phrases and long smooth ones.

4. Make an audiotape of your lines and listen to it over and over until you know your cues and your lines.

5. Make sure you understand what's going on in the scene. Each line must be said in a way that is consistent with other things your character says and does.

6. Have a family member or friend help you memorize your lines by reading the other characters' parts.

7. Look for key words in your lines that need to be stressed. This will help you to remember

   • words that start or end a sentence

   • the repetition of certain words

   • words that build an image through their meaning

## Enlisting "Angels"

During the week before the first performance, be prepared. The cast is nervous and excited and sometimes there can be irritations and short tempers. I usually ask two of the parents who are especially sympathetic listeners to be our "Angels." I announce to the cast that if there are any problems with other cast members to take their grievances to one of the Angels and not to me. All it takes is listening quietly to what the students have to say, and then asking the students what they think they should do about it. Usually all they need is to be heard with someone's full attention.

Any problem that arises is only as big as you make it. It's not a problem if you see it as an opportunity to create and learn.

During the week before the production I start each rehearsal with warm-up exercises, which includes the cast and crew shaking the hands of at least three cast members who usually don't hang out together. Then I tell them how spectacular they are as a group. This usually gets us going in the direction of cooperating with one another and feeling good about our goal.

As long as you stay organized, working on a production is exhilarating, exhausting, and one of the most rewarding projects you could ever do. It sounds like a lot, but remember: eating a twelve-course meal is enjoyable when done one bite at a time.

## The Job of the Director

The job of the director is to keep the entire production on track. The director oversees every aspect of the play so that a unified, cohesive whole comes out of the many separate parts. It is rewarding to see how all the different parts come together to create a beautiful production.

A good director also encourages ideas and tries to fully use all the talent that is present. When directing young people's theatre, remember: it is the students' play and their production. Therefore:

- Go with as many of their ideas as possible.
- Encourage their creativity and spotlight their talents.
- Stay organized and one step ahead so that things move smoothly.
- Be enthusiastic about their progress and what they are giving to the production.

"Help to deck her up." —*Romeo and Juliet*

# ■ ■ ■ 5 ■ The Production

## Production Committees

In our theatre company, most students participate in the production by both serving on a production committee and acting in some capacity. Each student chooses a technical area that he or she is interested in and signs up for one committee, choosing from:

- lights
- set
- costumes
- props
- stage crew
- publicity
- makeup

The lighting crew is the only production crew that cannot act in the play.

At the end of each section below, you will find a list of steps involved for each production area. These lists are reproduced in Appendix B, page 88, and may be photocopied and passed around to your students.

Every committee needs:

1. an adult mentor to help the students keep on track
2. a designated student to chair the group

### LIGHTS

Lights can be as simple or as complex as you make them. I suggest that you start with a simple plan. We have been fortunate—for two years we had a lighting instructor who trained an excellent light crew that keep coming back and doing a magnificent job.

If no one in your group is knowledgeable about lighting:

- Enter into the project in the spirit of learning together.
- Keep the lights simple.

- Find someone in your community theatre who can give you pointers.
- Go to the library and find books on lighting.
- Experiment together on lights and check out what works best.

To avoid equipment damage and to eliminate any possible injury to students, be sure you're introduced to the lighting capabilities in the theatre by a lighting expert. Stress safety first, as the students will be working with electricity and need to be aware of its potential dangers. Keep it simple to start with and add new tricks and techniques with each new production.

Some safety precautions:

1. Keep all the lighting equipment clean and free of dust.
2. Disconnect electrical equipment and make sure everything is properly fused and grounded.
3. Never try to mend anything with the power source on.
4. If you have questions, seek out a qualified electrician.

**Checklist for the Light Crew**

1. Make a list of the name and phone number of each member of the committee.
2. Read through the scenes in the play and make notes.
3. Check out what is available for lights with someone who is knowledgeable about the equipment. Remember: *Safety first!*
4. Meet with the director and review each scene.
5. Brainstorm on how to create appropriate lighting effects.
6. Learn how to use the lights to get the effects you want. Place an actor onstage and experiment with different angles and intensity.
7. Map out your lighting plan using the script.
8. Practice with the lights.
9. Keep a list of anything you borrow and return it promptly after the show.

10. Write thank-you notes to anyone who helped your committee.

## SET

The set committee needs to work closely with the director so that there is cohesiveness to the end product. If you keep the set simple, the students will be able to do most of the work.

### Flats

Learn to make flats. Flats are large frames (usually about nine feet tall by three feet wide) that are stretched with canvas, painted, and used for scenery backdrops. Take your time and construct good flats, because you can use them repeatedly if they are stored properly. Just paint over them for each new play. Instructions on building flats are included later in this chapter.

### Safety

When constructing platforms or stairs, ask an adult who is knowledgeable about construction. The set must never endanger in any way the actors or stage crew. Be sure everything is secured on the stage and that the set can be moved by the stage crew without anyone getting hurt.

### Stage Size

Depending on the size of your stage, the set needs to cover the area from top to bottom. We have worked on many different stages and each one presents its own challenges. Usually elementary schools have very small stages while high schools have larger ones. The set needs to fit the stage. Scale down the size of the flats if you are working on small stage areas.

### Creative Set Changes

Remember that the length of the scenes also dictates how elaborate or simple the set needs to be. Think of ways you can create scene changes with lights or simple props. For instance, a street scene can be portrayed by using a streetlight and a bench, or a garden scene can be set using a vine-entwined trellis.

Sometimes if you have an elaborate scene change following

a short scene, you can play the short scene in front of the curtain with a few props while the set change is quietly happening behind the curtain.

**Plan and Enlist Help**

Set design and construction takes a while, so be sure you give your set committee plenty of time to design, construct, and paint the scenes. Local community theatre people may help you get started. If needed, enlist the help of local artists and carpenters.

### Checklist for the Set Committee

1. Make a list of the name and phone number of each member of the committee.
2. Read through the play and list the different scenes and how many set changes there are.
3. Brainstorm about what you would like to do for each scene.
4. Meet with the director to go over ideas and make decisions.
5. Make a list of materials and tools you will need. Estimate the cost.
6. Get permission to purchase the materials, and have everything you need for each work period.
7. Agree on a construction schedule. Remember to give yourselves an extra hour for each work period to enable enough time for setup and cleanup.
8. Organize each work period so that each person on the committee has a job.
9. Make a list of all the steps required for the completion of each set.
10. Keep your work areas clean and orderly.
11. Keep a list of anything you borrow and return it promptly after the show.
12. Write thank-you notes to anyone who helped your committee.

## Instructions for Building Flats

Making a simple flat is a straightforward project that the students can do with some help from a knowledgeable adult.

### Materials

framing material (1" x 3" strapping)

plywood (for making small triangular gussets)

1" Sheetrock screws

$\frac{1}{4}$" staples

lightweight canvas or heavy-weight muslin

white glue

water

### Tools

saw

measuring tape

screw gun

carpenter's square

sharp craft knife

staple gun

Construct a frame that is nine feet tall by three feet wide. (See Figures 5–2 and 5–3 on pages 42–43.) Make sure the top and bottom pieces go the full three feet wide and butt the side pieces to them, joining them with the triangular plywood gussets. This is important for ease in sliding the flats across the stage.

Keep in mind that the gussets need to be screwed in about three-quarters of an inch from the outside edge using one-inch screws (this enables you to screw two flats together edge-to-face) to create a solid corner or a place to attach hinges, if you want a corner that can be placed at any angle on the stage.

To help support and strengthen the flat, add middle pieces using one-by-three-inch strapping and plywood gussets.

Next, stretch the muslin across the frame, starting at the middle and working your way out to either end. Pull the canvas around to the back side and staple, going from side to side and back and forth as you staple and stretch.

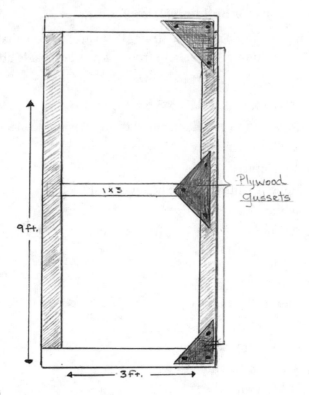

*Figure 5–2*

After stretching the muslin across the frame, mix a solution of white glue and water (one part glue to one part water) and paint it across the canvas. As it dries the muslin will be stretched across the flat for a tight, rigid fit.

Now the flat is ready to be painted and used for a backdrop. Flats are fairly lightweight and easy to slide on and off the stage, and there are endless possibilities of effects that can be made using them. Hinged together, two flats can be used to create easy backgrounds for short scenes.

Stored carefully, a good flat will last for many years. Just paint over the canvas or muslin each time you use it. Any flat latex paint will work.

## COSTUMES

First identify the time period of your play and what costumes are possible for each student to obtain without too much diffi-

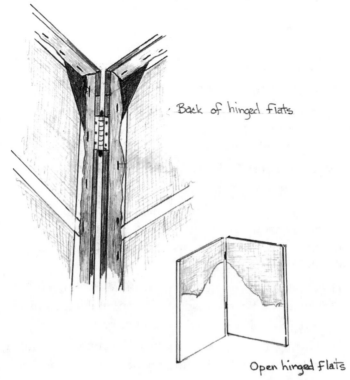

Back of hinged flats

Open hinged flats

*Figure 5–3*

culty. If you have a seamstress or two who are willing to help, you will be in good shape. If not, start seeking out good second-hand stores and gathering anything that will work. Often, some simple alterations and embellishments are all that's needed to create a perfect costume for little money. Remember to keep all the costumes clean and stored safely away from mice and moisture. Costumes can be used many times, and once you start collecting them the job of outfitting everyone gets easier each year.

As long as the costume committee works together, the work is enjoyable and rewarding. Be aware that if one person takes on too much, burnout will result.

### Checklist for the Costume Committee

1. Make a list of the name and phone number of each member of the committee.
2. List all the characters in the play and how many costume changes each has.

3. Meet with the director and brainstorm ideas.

4. List ideas for each character.

5. Be creative and resourceful; consider how much the cast can help.

6. Assign responsibility for specific costumes to each committee member.

7. Schedule times when you can go to secondhand clothing stores.

8. Get permission to purchase costumes or fabric.

9. Purchase a garment rack.

10. As you gather costumes, make a bag with each actor's name on it and keep the carefully folded costumes in the bags. Keep notes written on each bag of any work that needs to be done.

11. Expect to make changes to costumes after the first dress rehearsal. Do not be discouraged; making adjustments along the way is part of costuming.

12. During the course of the performances, remember to have an iron and ironing board set up in the changing room.

13. Keep a list of anything you borrow and make sure you clean it and return it promptly after the show.

14. Write thank-you notes to anyone who helped your committee.

## PROPS

The prop committee must first identify all the props needed for the play. To do this, read the play carefully and write down all the objects used during the performance. Next to each prop on the list, note what needs to be made and what needs to be purchased or borrowed. It is the responsibility of the committee to keep track of every prop and its source.

Organize all the props by scene and set up a prop table near the entrance to the stage. This is a sacred space. *No one* is to touch the props without permission. The stage manager is in charge of the prop table. Each actor is responsible for taking his or her prop onstage and placing it back on the prop table when he or she leaves the stage. Sometimes the actors are nervous and the stage manager needs to remind them of their prop. But most of the time the actors are right on top of what they need.

For *Romeo and Juliet* we made four swords, sheaths for the swords, and an old box camera on a tripod. For *Much Ado About Nothing* we made twenty-seven masks. Designing and constructing these kinds of props requires a lot of imagination. It takes a certain kind of mind to shine in this area, but that's the great thing about theatre: there is opportunity for everyone to be a star.

### Checklist for the Prop Committee

1. Make a list of the name and phone number of each member of the committee.
2. Read through the play and make a list of all the props needed for the play. Do this carefully.
3. Brainstorm about where you can get the props or how you can make them.
4. Meet with the director to go over all your ideas.
5. Create a budget and get permission to purchase props or materials to make them.
6. Give each student responsibility for a certain number of props.
7. Keep a list of anything you borrow, including the owner's name and telephone number.
8. Set up the prop table scene by scene.
9. Promptly return anything you borrowed with a thank-you note.
10. Write thank-you notes to anyone who helped the prop committee.

### STAGE CREW

Not everyone wants to be onstage. Some students are fascinated by the technical side of stage work. In our group, the stage crew gets a lot of appreciation, because without them we wouldn't have a show. It is important for the actors to understand this and to share the applause with them.

During production, the stage hands need to rehearse all scene changes so that everything runs smoothly during the performance. The crew shoulders much responsibility. They need to know exactly who moves what for each scene.

Rehearse the scene changes so that they are done quickly and quietly. Make sure the stage hands have lists for each change, so they know exactly where things go. Allot plenty of time to practice all changes.

The stage manager is in charge of all this and has the most responsibility of anyone during the performances. It is an enormous job. We have had student and adult stage managers. Both have worked out well. In our last production we had two adults who shared the job of stage manager, and that seemed to work out best.

Put some thought into who you ask to be stage manager. The position requires a leader who enjoys organizing people and gets along well with everyone. Stage managers need to know how to keep their cool in tight situations and to think quickly on their feet. A good stage manager is worth his or her weight in gold!

## Publicity

The publicity committee takes care of making and distributing posters, selling tickets, writing press releases and feature articles, supplying photographs to the newspaper, doing local radio show interviews, and creating the program guide, which may include selling ads to help defray printing costs. To ensure that each aspect is accomplished in a timely manner with sufficient lead time, a production schedule is necessary.

It is also important that the students on the publicity committee are old enough to write the news articles, and are articulate enough to do the radio interviews. The adult involved with this group must stay on top of things and remind the students of deadlines.

We have a contest every year to see who can sell the most tickets. It's a friendly contest with lots of joking around. Most of

"Let them signify under my sign."

the students sell quite a few tickets. This is a great way to get a full house. Anticipating a large audience builds enthusiasm.

### Checklist for the Publicity Committee

1. Make a list of the name and phone number of each member of the committee.

2. Read through the play and get a general idea about the story.

3. Meet with the director and brainstorm about a unified theme for all your publicity, and how to make posters, tickets, and programs.

4. Schedule a time for creating each item or assign each person on the committee to be in charge of one item.

5. Make a list of all materials and tools needed and create a budget.

6. Get permission to purchase materials.

7. Write articles/press releases for newspapers, create ads, schedule any interviews.

8. Distribute posters and assign one person to be in charge of ticket sales.

9. Write the program. Be sure you haven't forgotten anyone. Have an adult proofread it.

10. Sell ads to help pay printing costs.

11. Get the program printed the week before the show.

12. Write thank-you notes to anyone who helped the committee.

## MAKEUP

You will find the steps for applying makeup below. When we first started our theatre group, we used street makeup (basic foundation, lipstick, eyeliner, eye shadow, and rouge). Then we slowly began purchasing stage makeup. There is a big difference between the two. Stage makeup is more difficult to apply successfully; however, there is no end to the effects you can achieve when using it.

Do not fret too much over makeup; try to get everyone to learn how to apply his or her own. It's a great skill for actors and actresses to have. Remember, under stage lights, a face without makeup will appear totally washed out. All the actors and actresses need it.

### Steps for Applying Makeup

Straight stage makeup enlarges the features so that they are more vivid under the stage lights and from a distance. These are the basic steps to follow when applying makeup. Experiment when you need special effects such as an older character or a more fantastical creature.

1. Evenly spread foundation on the whole face and neck.

2. Use a darker brown foundation and apply it under the chin, along the jaw line on either side of the nose, and above the eyebrows. This gives shape to the face.

3. Use a pale highlighter on the cheekbones, down the center of the nose and above the jawbone.

4. Add rouge to cheeks, chin, and forehead.

5. Outline the eyes with eye pencil.

6. Apply eye shadow. For males, use a neutral color or brown; for females, use blue, green, or brown.

7. Apply lipstick. Males should use something close to their own lip color; females may use a deeper pink or red, depending on the role.

8. For the final effect, dust the entire face and neck with blending powder.

## Considerations

For sanitary reasons, tell the cast members to always gently wipe the end of a lipstick with tissue after they're done with it. Also ask them to bring their own eye pencils and mascara, as eye infections can be contagious.

Give the students some time to experiment with stage makeup. Many of the boys in our group do an excellent job applying their own makeup.

Look around the community for people who are knowledgeable about stage makeup techniques and invite them to give a demonstration to your group. It's a lot of fun to see the different effects makeup can achieve.

"When in other habits you are seen Orsino's mistress and his fancy's queen." —*Twelfth Night*

# ■ ■ ■ 6 ■ The Performance

## Getting Support from Parents

Encore has an agreement that if a child is involved with a play, one of his or her parents needs to contribute in some way. There is always something with which even a very busy parent can help. There are so many jobs that need to be done.

When Encore first started, I wanted the students to do all of the work, but it has evolved into a family theatre experience with parents and young people working side by side on the productions. The result has been a mutual respect between the young people and the adults. We are all amazed at the creativity that shines through every aspect of our productions. The whole process builds a sense of community, which I think is essential to leading meaningful lives.

Occasionally there is a parent who cannot be involved, but usually by the week before the performance we have not only all the mothers but most of the fathers helping. Many times after the play I receive heartfelt comments from parents telling me what it meant to them to have the opportunity to work with the young people and be involved in this exciting and creative process.

During the week before the first performance, we are at the theatre every night, and that gives many of the working parents a chance to be involved. The excitement that grows with each passing day is contagious. Many of the students tell me that the last week of the production is by far the best week of the entire school year for them. I would have to agree. When it's good, it's great.

Following is a list of jobs for parents that I have used over the years. I try to keep everything covered and anticipate trouble areas before they happen. We have a policy that every parent gets to see the play from the audience at least one time. It means juggling jobs backstage, but it's only fair.

**Jobs for Parents During the Performance**

1. Lines prompter. (Do not ask the stage manager to do this job; it should be one person's sole responsibility during the performance.)

2. Two or three people to style hair.

3. Costume helpers and checkers. Two or three adults to help with costume changes and to check each actor's costume before he or she goes onstage.

4. Two adults in the room backstage during the performance to help keep it quiet.

5. Repair seamstress, to walk around with scissors, thread, sewing needles, safety pins, et cetera to repair torn costumes or buttons that suddenly pop off.

6. Ticket seller.

7. An usher or two to hand out programs.

8. Two troubleshooters (usually fathers) who are willing to make themselves available just in case the unexpected happens. (Like having the curtain jump off its track just before the audience comes in.)

## The Week Before Opening Night

The week before the production is the most intense and exciting time. It can also be stressful, so it's important to keep everything in perspective.

First, be sure that the cast stays healthy and encourage everyone to take his or her vitamins, eat well, and get rest. I provide chamomile tea for anyone who wants to take a tea bag or two home. I suggest students drink a cup before going to bed to help them sleep. I do the same, as it works wonders for the nerves.

Be aware that many challenges will crop up all week. Utilize everyone's talents to overcome them. The director's job is not to solve all the problems (which would be impossible), but rather to keep the process moving forward and facilitate an atmosphere of cooperation and enthusiasm. Try to keep a good balance between being light enough to have fun and serious enough to put on a great show. Know the difference. Sometimes being the director means being the tough guy. As long as the students feel solid in their relationship with you, you can demand their best.

I try to keep everything moving by keeping a list of details on a clipboard, which I write down and check off with a pencil. We start each rehearsal with announcements. This is the time when each production committee chairperson updates us on the progress being made. It also gives everyone a chance to ask for anything he or she may need for the performance.

Time is always an issue as we get closer to opening night, so it's essential to keep things moving along. The last week keeps building in intensity. Stay in close contact with the assistant director, the music director if you have one, the light crew, and the stage manager.

The last week before a play, the director is in demand. If you are able to give yourself over to the job you will have a great time. The key to being a relaxed director is to take good care of yourself. Make sure you go for a daily walk, read something inspirational before you retire, eat well, and set aside a quiet time each day (even if it's only ten minutes).

I usually enjoy this part of the production because it gives all those involved an opportunity to show their strengths. I have been fortunate to receive a great deal of assistance during the last week before a performance, and the cast gives its all to the project. This is the "payoff" for having created a cohesive team of individuals who value themselves, one another, and the performance to which we have mutually committed.

## The Performance

The performance itself is a special time. It's what you have been working toward for the past few months. Ask the cast and crew to be at the theatre about two and a half hours before curtain time. That allows for just enough time to make any last-minute announcements, do some warm-ups together, and put on make-up and costumes.

When the cast and crew arrives at the theatre on opening night, I make sure that everyone is clear about what he or she is responsible for completing *before* the performance. The cast is nervous and excited and has the false sense of having a long

"By my troth, we that have good wits have much to answer for."
—*As You Like It*

time to get ready. I inform them that two and a half hours is not very much time to accomplish all the tasks necessary to be ready when the curtain opens.

Next we do our warm-up exercises, which consist of the body stretches and voice exercises described in Chapter 2. It is important to loosen up, which enables us to focus on our performance. While everyone is still together, have each person turn to a partner and shake his or her hand while saying something positive about him or her. Continue to do this with two or three other people and end in a big group hug. This facilitates good feelings between people and solidifies team effort.

Make sure you have someone videotape the performance. The students will get a big charge out of watching it. It also can be used as a tool for positive critiquing, but should be done in a spirit of lighthearted fun with the goal being to see how you might improve your performance next season.

**Checklist of Jobs That Need to Be Done Before Curtain Time**

Tech crew: Check lights.
Check set.
Check sound equipment.

Stage crew: Check props.
Check curtain.
Make sure all set changes are in order.

Musicians: Check to make sure instruments are in tune.
Check any amps or speakers.
Make sure sheet music is in order.

Makeup: Get everyone's makeup on.

Actors: Make sure everyone knows when to get onstage.
Go over anything with the really young students, and make sure there is a parent who is with them backstage during the performance.

Director: Be available to help anywhere it's needed.
Keep announcing the time.
Make sure the theatre is clean.
Do makeup checks under stage lights. (You must have everyone in makeup and checked before the audience comes.)
Close curtain thirty minutes before the performance and open the doors to the theatre. (I never let anyone in the audience see an actor before the performance. It's a good tool for building anticipation.)
Check with stage manager to make sure everything is ready to go.

Check with musicians.

Pull the entire cast, crew, and parents into a
room backstage and give them a last-
minute inspirational pep talk. (Encore has a
tradition in which we all make a circle and
cross our right hand over our left hand and
hold the little finger of the person next to
us. I give a short speech and then I start by
squeezing the little finger of the person to
my left and then he squeezes the finger of
the person next to him and the squeeze is
passed around the room until it gets back to
me. Everyone is perfectly silent and when
the squeeze is returned full circle, I look up
and say "One, two, three . . ." and everyone
yells "Break a leg!"

My job as the director is over at this point. I usually watch
the performance from the back of the auditorium with a headset
on that is hooked into the musicians, the light technicians, and
the stage manger. When I see something like the curtain not
opened far enough or the lights being too dim, I whisper into my
headset for it to be fixed.

I always feel nervous and excited, and watch the performance from the back of the theatre so that I can jump up and
pace around without disturbing anyone. I love watching the performance and seeing the reaction of the audience from the back.
We usually have very supportive audiences and sometimes the
students get standing ovations, which they work very hard for.

After the cast and crew have bowed and the curtains have
closed, I encourage them to come out into the audience. Many of
the people in the audience stay so that they can talk to the actors,
and that's where the power of theatre is most evident on the
faces of the cast and crew. Everyone deserves to hear how wonderful his or her contribution was to the performance.

It takes a while for everyone to wind down, so we get
cleaned up and usually someone gets ice cream and we all eat it
together and then we go home and try to sleep.

"Thou didst smile."

## FINAL WORDS FOR DIRECTORS

Believe in your cast and crew, and let them know how impressed you are with them. We have been through some pretty tight spots together: times where a cast member got so sick she couldn't perform and we had less than a day to fill her spot; times when a minor automobile accident prevented one of the main players from showing up. But the show must go on, and all that training in the beginning of the year pays off in confidence and skill during a performance.

The thing I always try to keep in mind is to have fun and to love everyone I'm working with. All of us have our strengths and weaknesses, and it's up to the director to set the tone by encouraging the strengths and minimizing the weaknesses. Never criticize anyone in the cast or the crew; they are trying their best with the abilities they have. Most of us are fully aware of our weaknesses, and no one thrives on criticism.

Enjoy the performance. It is a gift that the cast and crew

give to the audience, and it is especially gratifying for the director, because you know how much the students have put into it.

## The Cast Party

The cast party is an important part of the entire theatre experience. Some of the most wonderful memories of my life are of
exceptional cast parties. There is much to celebrate. Because it is
so important, take the time to plan and organize it.

There are three main elements of Encore's cast parties:

1. Dancing
2. Good food
3. Appreciating those individuals who were in charge of
   the production

For our first cast party, we hired a couple of contradance
musicians who called dances. Everyone loved it and we have
had contradances at every cast party since. It's a terrific way to
bring the families together to celebrate.

We have since formed our own contradance band and
caller, learning about the various dance steps and organizing
dances of our own. What a great way to get teens to party
together in a safe atmosphere! Anyone can contradance, and
often it's the beginners who have the most fun.

The second element of the cast party is the food. Keep it
simple by making it potluck. Organize it so that one group
brings chips and appetizers, one main dishes, and the other
desserts. Encourage people to bring lots of food and juice, soda,
and water. Make sure there is plenty of ice. After dancing everyone heads for the drinks.

The third element, and the one I like the best, is a time during the party when we all gather into one room and I single out
the individuals who helped produce the show—all the students
who chaired committees and all the parents who helped. This is
a time when I get to show my appreciation for all the behind-the-
scenes work that has been done. I give thank-you cards to each
parent and present a small framed certificate of appreciation to
each student leader.

The cast party is the stuff of which rich memories are made. It is a time for families to come together and appreciate the theatre community we have created and to celebrate our unique qualities.

## The Closing Ceremony

Letting a production go is the most difficult part of the entire process. Once it's gone it will never return. All the students, the props, the set, and the costumes get scattered to the winds. In the early years the Encore students really struggled with this part of the process. There was—and still is—a real letdown time for a week or two after the performance ended.

One of the ways I deal with this is to give it closure by bringing all the students together and telling them individually what unique contributions they made and how important they were to the success of the entire program. It is important to acknowledge our children. If their strengths and talents are appreciated by someone other than their parents, they get the message that out in the "big world" they have value. I always say something to each one about his future and how much I believe in him.

Then we hold hands and form a circle and sing one of the songs from the performance and say goodbye with hugs and tears. I remind them one last time to truly love one another and always reach out and be there for each other. For some, this performance will mark the beginning of lifelong friendships; for all it will be an experience they will carry throughout their lives.

This is an important time for me as well, because it is just as difficult. I have an especially hard time saying goodbye to the young people who are graduating and leaving for college or work. I get very attached to these students and love them dearly. I have stayed in touch with many of the older ones. In fact, every year during the last week of production, many of the alumni come back to see us, and they almost always come back for our performances and cast parties. We affectionately call them the Encore Alumni.

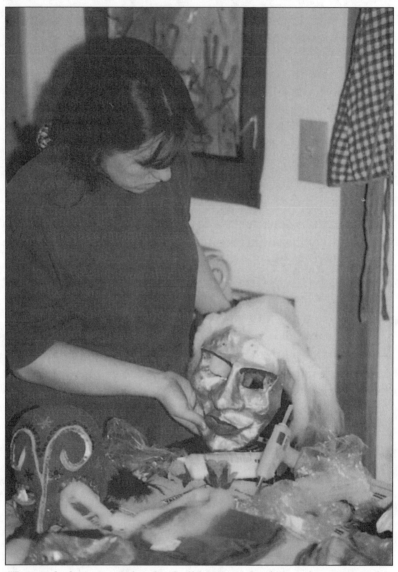

"For such disguise as haply shall become the form of my intent."
—*Twelfth Night*

# ■ ■ ■ 7 ■ More Theatre-Related Activities

## Mask Making

There are many kinds of masks you can make for all sorts of creative activities onstage. (See discussion of mask work in the section on body movement in Chapter 3.) Here are some ideas for how to make simple masks.

### PLASTER RIGID-WRAP MASKS

Rigid wrap is plaster-coated gauze that can be bought in craft shops or medical-supply stores. It is used for making casts to set broken limbs. You can employ rigid wrap to create masks, using your face as a form. This mask-making technique makes a permanent and beautiful creation that can be used for many productions.

**Materials**
bowl of lukewarm water
plastic bags
rigid wrap
plastic wrap
acrylic paints
sequins, ribbons, feathers, fabric, etc.
varnish
one-quarter-inch elastic
foam rubber

**Tools**
scissors
paintbrushes
sponges
stapler
glue gun
sandpaper

**Instructions**

This activity takes at least two sessions to complete one mask for each student who participates. Each student picks a partner. For the first half of the workshop one student will lie down and the other will use the first student's face for a form, then they will switch places.

**Session I**

1. Make a comfortable place for each student to lie down. (We usually place old bath towels on the floor for them to lie on.) Make sure that they are comfortable and that their hair is pushed back away from their face.

2. Have scissors, rigid wrap (cut into strips about one or two inches wide and six to twelve inches long), and a medium-sized bowl of lukewarm water ready on the floor beside each participant.

3. Turn on some good music (for fun).

4. Cut a plastic bag open and carefully place it over the student's face, marking a place for the nostrils and the mouth. Immediately remove the plastic and cut a hole for the mouth and two small holes for the nostrils, then place it back over the student's face.

5. Place the rigid-wrap strips (two or three at a time) into the water.

6. Starting at the forehead, layer the rigid wrap across the face from temple to temple. Overlap the layers and smooth out each one with your fingertips, being very gentle, especially around the eyes.

7. Continue layering the face until it is completely covered and smooth.

8. Now add two or three more layers until you feel that the mask, when dry, will be sturdy.

9. Wait about five minutes after adding the last layer of wet strips, then carefully lift it from the face.

10. Set it on a table (covered with plastic wrap) to dry and harden.

11. Ask the students to switch places and begin the process on their partner.

12. Allow the masks to dry overnight.

Whenever I have taught this mask-making technique, it has been enormously successful. It has a soothing effect on both students. (It was great to watch some of the more aggressive students be so gentle when making masks using their partner's face.)

**Session II**

For the second session, cover worktables with newspaper and set out paints, glue guns, sequins, ribbons, fabric, feathers, and anything else you can think of to decorate the masks. When the students arrive, match each mask to the person whose face formed it, put on some jazzy music, and let them create.

1. Apply paint to the front of the mask.

2. After the paint has dried—but before gluing on any embellishments—a coat of varnish needs to be applied.

3. Varnish takes only a short while to dry, so use this time to clean up any paintbrushes and paints. Try to stay ahead of the mess so that there is plenty of room to create.

4. When the varnish has dried, glue the feathers, sequins, and ribbons to the mask.

5. When the masks are completed, glue and staple an elastic band to the back.

6. Check to see if there are any rough spots on the inside of the mask. If so, use a little sandpaper to smooth it out, or cut small strips of foam rubber measuring about one-quarter inch thick, and glue pieces to the inside of the mask around the edges.

## PAPIER-MÂCHÉ MASKS

This beautiful and lightweight mask can be created from papier-mâché using wet clay as the form. If stored properly, the masks may be used for years to come.

**Materials**

Masonite boards (one per mask)
clay (can be purchased from a craft supply shop or a local
    potter)
plastic wrap
newspaper or brown paper bags (grocery bags)
white glue
water
acrylic paints
varnish
ribbons, sequins, feathers, etc.
foam rubber
one-quarter-inch elastic

**Tools**

old container for mixing glue and water
paintbrushes
sponges
scissors
glue gun
stapler
sandpaper

**Instructions**

This activity will take about three and a half hours to complete.
It will have to be done in two sessions as the papier-mâché will
take a few days to dry before it can be embellished. It's always
fun to have music playing while the students are making their
masks.

**Session I**

1. Ahead of time have an adult who is adept with a table
   saw cut Masonite boards into squares measuring eighteen inches along each side. You will find many uses for
   these boards if you keep them clean. Masonite makes
   great outdoor drawing boards, craft activity boards, or
   lap desks.

2. Give each student a lump of clay big enough to make a
   mold about the size of a human face (measure their faces
   for length and width). The clay on the board should have

a depth of about five inches, which includes the form of the nose.

3. Suggest various possibilities without giving the students too many ideas. For instance, the facial features could be accentuated by creating a very large nose, or heavy, thick brows, or perhaps a beak in place of a nose. This mask-making technique is so flexible because the students are working with wet clay. Make sure that the length and width of the mask will fit their face.

4. After they are satisfied with their clay form, wrap the form in plastic wrap, being careful to cover the clay completely.

5. Tear newspaper (or brown grocery bags) into one- to two-inch-wide strips and make a mixture of glue and water in a bowl (one and a half parts glue to one part water). Dip each strip into the solution and carefully lay each one onto the form.

6. Repeat until there are about four layers of papier-mâché.

7. Smooth down each layer and crisscross the strips so that the mask will have added strength. This will take between two to four days to dry while on the mold.

8. When dry, carefully remove the mask from the mold and let it air out for at least a day before painting.

**Session II**

1. Set up a work space for the next class by covering the worktables with newspaper and set out the paint, varnish, and other decorative embellishments.

2. Remember to varnish the mask after painting it and before gluing anything to it.

3. When the varnish has dried, glue the feathers, sequins, ribbons, or whatever decorative items are desired, to the mask.

4. When the masks are completed, glue and staple the elastic band to the back.

5. Check to see if there are any rough spots on the inside of the mask. If so, use a little sandpaper to smooth it out, or

cut small strips of foam rubber measuring about one-quarter-inch thick, and glue pieces to the inside of the mask around the edges.

6. Attach an elastic band around the back.

## Paper Masks

Using poster board and Magic Markers is the easiest and quickest way to make masks.

### Materials
poster board
Magic Markers
glue
tape
elastic
ribbons, sequins, feathers, stickers, gold stars, etc.

### Tools
sharp scissors
stapler
hole punch

### Instructions

1. Precut a simple oval shape and pass around to each student.

2. Have each student cut out the mouth, eyes, and nose for each mask.

3. Set out all the adornments and markers and encourage them to create.

We have experimented with cutting out various shapes to create masks that are three dimensional. For instance, cut a triangular hole big enough for the nose in the center of the mask. Using another piece of cardboard, cut a triangle about twice the size of the nose opening. Bend the triangle into a nose shape and tape it over the hole on the mask.

When you have completed your mask, punch a small hole on each side near the eye openings using the hole punch. Lace the elastic through the holes and staple the elastic together. Now you have a way to wear the mask.

With scissors, tape, and glue, you can do some extraordinary work. Just have plenty of poster board on hand and go for it. Don't be annoyed by any waste of materials, as it takes experimentation to figure out three-dimensional shapes. Set aside the rejects and encourage creative exploration.

## A FINAL WORD ABOUT MASKS

If your cast will be dancing or running onstage while wearing masks, you will want to design the masks for ease of breathing. We have created some outstanding masks, using all three methods, that only cover the upper half of the face. One year we made bird masks that covered the eyes, and the nose was formed into a beak. We glued feathers and sequins to them and the effect was stunning!

# *Mime*

## BASIC ELEMENTS OF MIME

Mime is a beautiful performing art that uses gestures and actions and is usually accomplished without words. It concentrates on body movement. Mimes can be metaphorical and poetic in their presentation. They can be performed to music or in absolute silence. Simple close-fitting costumes work best.

There are three main elements to keep in mind when creating a mime. Emphasize the following points.

1. A mime, like a good skit, tells a story. It has a beginning, a middle, and an end. Ideally the end has a punch to it like a good poem. Mimes can be funny or tragic. The best ones are fairly short in duration. Remember that you need to keep the attention of the audience, so keep the action going.

2. Slow down your movements and accentuate them. Use your hands in different ways and move each part of your body with mindfulness. Practicing in front of a mirror is helpful.

3. Keep the set, costumes, and props simple. Some of the most powerful mimes are done in front of the black traveler (the back curtain) onstage. Props can be used, but

"The web of our life is of mingled yarn."

—*All's Well That Ends Well*

often objects themselves are pantomimed. Costuming should contrast with the background so that the body is at all times the main focus.

### AN EXAMPLE OF A GREAT MIME

One of the most wonderful mimes I have ever seen was created and performed by two Encore students. It consisted of a lonely soul walking on the stage. He had a clear vinyl pocket sewn on his shirt. In the pocket was a bright red heart.

He had his hands over his heart in order to protect it. Each time he was given a chance to give of his heart he refused. He became stingier and more miserable as he went along until finally he came upon a situation in which he tentatively gave from his heart and at once was transformed into a joyous human being.

That mime was a touching and beautiful experience for everyone watching. Even the young students were mesmerized by the movements and the message.

## *Storytelling*

### BASIC ELEMENTS OF STORYTELLING

We all love stories. Since the beginning of human time, people have been enthralled by storytellers. Good stories contain rich and many-colored threads that can weave together a tapestry of the human spirit across the generations. Whether funny, sad, or poignant, the most powerful teachings are taught through stories.

Explain to your students that there are four tools that storytellers hone: voice, body, mind, and heart.

### Voice

Finding one's own voice takes a while, sometimes years. Emphasize the importance of clear enunciation and voice projection. How a tale is told is as important as the story itself. Remind the students that the quality of their voice can hold or repel an audience and that doing voice exercises helps in the development of a storyteller. (See section on voice training in Chapter 3.)

### Body

Point out to the students the importance of body movement and body language in storytelling. Give them examples of how they can stand and tell a story using gestures to pantomime the action, or they can sit and use their hands to emphasize key elements. They can also use clapping their hands or tapping their feet for sound effects or for keeping rhythm during a lively story. Playing a musical instrument and using it for a prop can also add interest to the tale.

### Mind

We use our intelligence in every aspect of storytelling, from finding a story we want to tell, to thinking quickly on our feet when telling it. Storytelling draws on our creativity. Explain to the students that it takes focused attention for the storyteller to capture an audience and to weave them into his or her spell. Improvisation work is excellent training for storytelling. The one telling the story often draws on his or her past to add emotional depth to each tale.

Storytelling is not just for children. It can be a powerful tool for concerned adults to illustrate an important life lesson to teenagers without it running the risk of sounding like the dreaded lecture.

### Heart

Explain to the students that if a story doesn't have heart, it's missing a vital ingredient. Stories that connect people through common themes, experiences, or emotions, are stories with heart. If a story doesn't make us laugh, or think, or feel deeply, it's a missed opportunity. Tell the students that a mean-spirited story that pokes fun at someone is a lie, and not to waste a precious moment of their lives telling one.

That is not to say that in a good story there isn't lying, cheating, or stealing—but these things must be portrayed truthfully. All good stories have a moral ending, even if the tale is about immoral characters.

The basic elements in a good story are listed below.

1. It has a beginning, middle, and end.
2. There is conflict.
3. The characters are developed and believable.
4. There is rising tension.
5. There is a climax.
6. There is resolution and an ending.

### Exercise

Give the students an introduction to storytelling and ask them to find a story, develop it, and come to the next class prepared to present it. It can be a family story, a legend, a tall tale, or a comedy. Anything goes, as long as it is appropriate for the age level. Also, be prepared to tell one yourself. Use the introduction to help students become aware of the elements of good storytelling, and then sit back and enjoy!

## *Playwriting*

### BASIC ELEMENTS OF PLAYWRITING

Getting students to write is often a challenge. One of the most exciting ways to motivate them is to give them the opportunity to see their writing performed onstage. Playwriting is an art worthy of another book, but here is enough to get you started.

To simplify the process, start with scripts. Explain the format in which a script is written. Find two or three scripts to illustrate your point. Without getting too hung up on form, get them started with the basics. Whatever form you use, emphasize that ease of reading out loud is extremely important.

On a blackboard make an easy-to-follow form the students can use. For example, each speaker is identified by name, which is usually placed in the left-hand margin in capital letters. The dialogue is in regular type, written to the right of the name, while the stage direction is italicized in parentheses. Like this:

ROMEO: What light through yonder window breaks? It is the east and Juliet is the sun.
*(Hides behind bush stage left)*

Basically, a play has three elements: (1) characters who dialogue and move, or are moved by, (2) the action of (3) the story. Discuss the elements of a good story (see previous section). Talk about skits that have been presented that were especially good, and ask what made them so entertaining. Before the students write, point out the aid of answering "the five W's and one H": who, what, where, when, why, and how.

*Who* refers to the characters. *What* describes the action and the conflict(s). *Where* and *when* refer to the setting or location of the play and its time period. *Why* goes to the meaning or purpose of the story and the motivation of the characters. *How* refers to the manner in which conflicts develop and get resolved and in what way the characters interact to move the story along.

Emphasize the dialogue and the action. The dialogue needs to be natural and flow the way it does in real life, conversationally. The action needs to be not only realistic (or at least believable), but also exciting to watch. Review the basics and then let the students dive in. They will learn more about scriptwriting by doing it than by listening to a teacher talk about it.

While there are many different ways to approach a class on scriptwriting, here's one way we have used successfully. Divide students into small groups of four or five and make sure each group of students has a separate area away from the others in which to work. Ask them to create a skit by doing the following:

1. Brainstorm and write down ideas for characters and action. (five minutes)
2. Build a story out of the ideas. (ten minutes)
3. Write the dialogue. (ten to fifteen minutes)
4. Read it out loud and rewrite. (ten minutes)
5. Choose the parts. (two to three minutes)
6. Rehearse briefly. (five to ten minutes)
7. Perform it for the class while reading the script.

Ask the students to give full attention to each group's performance. This class usually lasts a couple of hours; if needed it could be done in two consecutive periods. Once the students have a format to follow (make a simple handout they can take home) ask them to write a script on their own for the next class. Have them make enough copies of their scripts so that their plays can be performed by their classmates.

During the second class, students who want to have their script performed can do so, by asking their classmates to read the different parts. Give the group about ten minutes to rehearse and then start the performances. Discussing each script and performance can be encouraging for the playwrights as long as the comments are helpful and positive.

Understanding and participating in the process of scriptwriting will provide a greater appreciation for master playwrights and good plays. If you approach it as a hands-on learning experience and immerse them in the process, the students will learn in a meaningful way and chances are they will retain the knowledge. The power of theatre work is in the process of being personally engaged.

"Be clamorous and leap all civil bounds rather than make unprofited returns." —*Twefth Night*

# ▪ ▪ ▪ 8 ▪ Shakespeare

## *What a Guy!*

Before I started Encore, I had positive exposure to Shakespeare in high school and college . . . but only exposure. I had read *Romeo and Juliet, Julius Caesar, Macbeth,* and *Hamlet* for various assignments. I had a high school English teacher who helped us through *Romeo and Juliet* with enthusiasm, but I hardly knew enough to teach Shakespeare to a drama group. In the spirit of learning something new, I read and reread various plays, watched films, attended stage performances, and talked to people who had a profound understanding of the Bard.

After directing our first Shakespearean play I was absolutely stunned by the beauty of Shakespeare. My poet heart took wing. It was a true epiphany for me and I've never looked back.

I remember struggling with Shakespeare in high school, trying hard to understand what was being said. The Encore students have never struggled with it in the same way. Rather, they wrestle with it, chew on it, debate different ways to deliver a line or flesh out a character. They have been performing, reading, and watching Shakespeare for the past several years and they love it! No one told them it was intimidating.

Of course, there are different levels of understanding Shakespeare. The six-to-ten-year-olds are engrossed in the plot or story line, the early adolescents are starting to develop insight into character, and by the time they are older teenagers they are diving into the motivation of the characters, the double meanings of many of the lines, the subtleties of the poetry, the texture of the scenes, the building of the story, and transforming each character through their own intelligence. Not only can they follow the story line but they are also able to dig into the deeper layers of Shakespeare and come up feeling well fed and satisfied.

Shakespeare is always true to the universal truth of being human. He does not distort, twist, or manipulate truth. His characters are, by and large, extremely complex, interesting and many-faceted jewels, each one worthy of a semester of study.

When I asked my husband why he thought Shakespeare, who lived nearly four hundred years ago (1564–1616), was still being performed today, he answered that it was because Shakespeare had his hand on the pulse of humanity. In the Bard's vivid portrayal of human nature there are powerful lessons for young people. There is every kind of evil character in Shakespeare's plays, which gives young people the opportunity to examine moral dilemmas and the consequences of immoral behavior. There are characters of good and evil, ones that stand strong and don't fall into temptation and characters who innocently do wrong. There are fools, and foolishness, impulsive actions, and consequences that cause great suffering. By the end of each tragedy, justice prevails. In each comedy everything comes full circle. And the plays still apply today, written by an author who lived four centuries ago.

## Making Shakespeare Accessible

There are a number of resources available to help you make Shakespeare accessible to young people. (See the Resources section for recommended material.) There are children's books available about Shakespeare and his works, edited scripts, Cliffs Notes, and videos of his plays, which can be a great help.

When first introducing a play it is important to give an overview of the story line so that students can follow along, then, if possible, go see a performance (or watch a movie) to help bring the story to life.

There are some excellent contemporary videos of Shakespearean plays. The actor and director Kenneth Branagh has done ingenious work in films of Shakespeare's plays. Sir Laurence Olivier's classic movies of Shakespearean plays have endured and can be rented from many video stores. There are also videos available of stage productions through the Canadian Broadcasting Corporation.

Some of the contemporary film versions of Shakespeare, in

my opinion, take too many liberties and dilute the integrity of the work. But this can be a useful tool with the students. We have had some spirited discussions on the contemporary films and I am excited to hear their opinions on some of the newer versions.

Students benefit most from seeing a stage performance. I think Shakespeare is to be watched first and read second. After an introduction to the story, watching a performance and then reading it is an excellent way for young people to grasp the work. But nothing compares to an actual performance by the students themselves.

In the Western world, Shakespeare is considered the master playwright. He has stood the test of time, and for good reason. An understanding of Shakespeare not only provides a solid foundation for appreciating theatre, whether as a professional or as an educated audience, but the story lines and famous dialogue are an integral part of cultural literacy. Why not join in and discover the immense richness of theatre through the master? Not only will your life be enriched by the experience, but so will the lives of your students and their audience.

## Teens and Shakespeare

During the adolescent years, every young person changes dramatically. Their bodies blossom and are redefined, their voices change, their thoughts deepen, and their emotions go haywire. This is a critical stage of development. With tremendous family support and healthy relationships, the teen years can be transformational in a positive way; without it these years can be devastating. Without the opportunity to fully grow emotionally and intellectually into manhood or womanhood, a twenty-one-year-old is only adult in body, not in maturity. A full-grown adult with a child's perspective on life often creates dangerous and heartbreaking situations.

These are the years when a lot of attention to sharpening moral awareness is crucial. Strong adult presence is needed in each teenager's life. A mentor or two is vital. Opportunities to engage in real-life work with responsibility are pivotal to a young person's development. Gaining a deeper awareness of relationships and human strengths and weaknesses will serve them well.

Shakespeare has the potential to wake up and shake the soul of emerging adults and crack their childhoods up against life in a theatre setting. Sounds pretty dramatic?

In all the years I have worked with the process of combining Shakespeare and teenagers, I have been amazed at the intensity of spirit and soul that students bring to the performance. Shakespeare has everything for teens: wise men, fools, hysterics, witches, lovers, mischief makers, evildoers, greed, rage, compassion, humor, love—and it's all written in iambic pentameter!

Our teens love knowing that they are performing something as difficult and respected as Shakespeare. As they bring the Bard's words to life, they have an outlet for those emerging raw emotions, which can be focused onstage in a way that is safe and receives applause and appreciation from an audience. What a tremendous release, to realize that stored-up emotions can be used for other things besides lashing out at friends and family members! All that energy can be channeled into a project requiring passion and intensity to succeed.

I have stumbled upon a powerful tool for teens: Shakespeare! Although traditionally taught in schools, it is mostly made as boring as possible, presented as having been written in archaic language by some dead stiff who lived four hundred years ago. But the key in bringing these timeless stories and words to life is in how it's taught. Don't read it, perform it! Chew on it, figure it out, let the poetry roll off the tongue and into the hearts of those emerging adults we call adolescents.

"We are such stuff as dreams are made on."

# ■ ■ ■ 9 ■ The Power of Theatre with, by, and for Young People

## Awakening to the World of Theatre

When I first started working with young people in theatre arts, I had no clue as to how powerful an impact the experience would have on them. I have witnessed total transformations in children as they go from shyly being onstage during a crowd scene, to playing major parts in our productions. I have watched awkward children turn into graceful dancers; ones who barely speak sing beautifully to a full house; and students who have been labeled learning-disabled learn long Shakespearean soliloquies and deliver them with meaning and grace.

No one was more amazed at the impact than I. To say I was delighted is an understatement. I often came home from rehearsals shaking my head in disbelief at what the young people were accomplishing. Their intensity of focus and their commitment to the production has always been inspiring. Their earnest efforts, and belief in me as their director, has reignited my own excitement for theatre work. Enthusiasm is contagious. There is nothing quite like working with the vitality of young people.

### THE SHY CHILD

There are many quiet children who only dream of being involved with stage work. I have found the shy ones to be the most sensitive and considerate young people. Go slowly with these students; the process will bring them from the shadow of their shyness into the confident glow of the limelight. Always encourage them, finding something that they do well. Find and nurture a strength that could be capitalized on for a future production.

Like most teachers, I often see potential in students of which they themselves are unaware. If we reach them through theatre experience, we help them tap into their own greatness. A shy child is usually a personality type that is self-conscious and fearful of ridicule. Create a safe environment and you will find them growing bold enough to participate fully in the experience.

## THE OUTSPOKEN CHILD

There is at least one outspoken individual in every group. Theatre, by its nature, attracts the more aggressive, outgoing students whose natural inclinations are to compete against each other for stage time. Be sensitive to their feelings, but also let them know that theatre is not a competitive sport.

One thing that helps tone down some of the more aggressive types is to have them play quiet roles; roles that require them to portray shy, sensitive people. This may well be the first time these students have even thought about what it's like to wear another person's shoes.

Outspoken students can be a lot of fun, are easy to chum around with, and add a wonderful dynamic to the group. Always encourage each student to keep the energy positive and be considerate of others.

## THE TEEN WHO PUSHES THE ENVELOPE

Actually, most teens are trying to push the envelope. This can be an exciting time for a young person. It can also be a time of confusion, doubt, and extreme behavior. What I have found working with teens is this: the more responsibility that is placed upon them, the more focused they become.

It's pretty simple, but something we seem to have forgotten: teens need meaningful work in the real world. Work that is physically demanding, intellectually stimulating, and challenges their creativity. Respect their developing opinions and encourage them to express themselves articulately. Help them gain self-confidence by praising their efforts. Point out their emerging strengths and support them. Remember to listen more than you speak. While you run the risk of having your heart broken, there is nothing quite as rewarding as having a good, mutually respectful relationship with a young person.

## Honoring the Intelligence of the Group

Try to remember what is important. It is not the perfect performance of a play, or taking the production to Broadway, or gaining international acclaim for excellence in theatre work. It is the young people with whom you are working.

The important element in theatre work is relationships, and encouraging the students to be their best. It's about how to work together, play together, and be together as a community of caring individuals of all ages. Helping everyone to tap into their own creativity, and giving their ideas to the spotlight, is the key to a successful production. The important element in the whole process is love. Love for the work and love for one another.

Do not undervalue the group's intelligence by asking them to produce a play that lacks substance or is a waste of their talents and abilities. Reach for the stars. Encourage them to go one step beyond what they think they can do.

Begin with something simple that is not over ninety minutes in length, and let the ideas fly. Add your special effects, let the actors bring their insights to their roles, and grow together as you learn theatre arts. Each year Encore Young People's Stage Company tackles a bigger production than the year before. Give your players enough of a challenge to stretch, but be realistic. Set up your group for success and choose a play that will give everyone an opportunity to grow and mature.

## Giving Everyone a Chance

Give everyone a chance to be onstage. About halfway through every production, a few students who were too shy to audition will say that they wish they could have a line or two in the play. My philosophy is: Anyone who wants a part will have a part; even if I have to write one.

To accommodate the actors, I have sometimes changed Shakespeare's characters from male to female parts or added a servant or two with some lines. I have even taken a large part and cut it in two so that there are enough parts to go around. That's the beauty of Shakespeare. His work is public domain and we can do pretty much what we want with it. I do not change his words, but I will edit them or move things around to fit our stage company.

We also add music and dancing to the plays because I want the students to develop in those areas as well. The big production numbers are a way to get everyone working together and having a great time.

Be sure the same students don't always get the big parts. Even if you have weaker talent, get them onstage. As you work with them, they will get stronger through the rehearsals and pull it off beautifully. It may take extra work on your part but it is worth the effort to see that student sparkle under the stage lights.

When you see a weak spot in a scene, single it out and go over it a few times until the actors get it right. Take the time to gather their insights and personal styles into the characters they are portraying. Give everyone a chance to shine and the production will illuminate the stage.

## *"All the World's a Stage"*

In our public schools today we voice our concern about self-esteem and search for experiences that can empower students. We need look no further than the auditoriums and stages almost every public school in this country possess.

This is a time when the arts are being financially challenged and school programs are being stretched to their limits. Our young people are growing up in an environment that can be morally degrading, undermining the values that most parents want to instill in their children.

Theatre is a noncompetitive way to explore our human nature, to seek truth, and to strive for excellence. It offers a way to dialogue with teens and encourage sensitivity and deeper levels of thinking. It is a way to teach English, history, art, music, and physical education in a manner that engenders lifelong interest in learning and will never be forgotten.

We at Encore Young People's Stage Company have gone through a metamorphosis. Our wings are drying in the sun and we are readying ourselves to take flight into our next production, whether it be a Shakespearean play or life itself, because, for us, "All the world's a stage!"

# Appendix A: Theatre as a Relevant Curriculum

The following subjects are covered in-depth through theatre work:

English:     Reading and analyzing plays
              Playwriting and playwrights

History:     Historical background of the setting and characters
              Historical background of the playwright

Math:     Set construction
              Stage layout
              Lighting techniques
              Making stage models
              Accounting/fiscal management (budgeting)

Science:     Electrical engineering
              Lighting techniques
              The structural strengths of various materials used
                 for set construction
              How to achieve various special effects

Music:     Reading music
              Playing instruments
              Singing

Fine Art:     Painting scenes
              Creating props
              Designing costumes
              Designing sets

Shop:     All woodworking techniques and acquired skills

Physical
Education:     All body movement including dance, acrobatics,
                 and stage stunts
              Choreographing scene changes
              Warm-up exercises
              All set and stage construction

Speech:     Public speaking
              Enunciation
              Voice projection

**Theatre work is a vital avenue for developing the following skills:**

- motor coordination
- hand/eye coordination
- following directions
- active listening
- articulating ideas clearly
- spatial perception
- memorization
- enunciation
- interpersonal communication
- reading and writing
- organizational skills
- teamwork

**Theatre work also enables students to:**

- build confidence
- learn acting techniques
- appreciate the complexity of the performing arts
- learn production techniques
- interact with their community
- learn public speaking
- have an opportunity to find their creative voice
- become more perceptive
- learn to cooperate with others in a noncompetitive environment

# Appendix B:
# Production Area Checklists

## Checklist for the Light Crew

☐ 1. Make a list of the name and phone number of each member of the committee.

☐ 2. Read through the scenes in the play and make notes.

☐ 3. Check out what is available for lights with someone who is knowledgeable about the equipment. Remember: *Safety first!*

☐ 4. Meet with the director and review each scene.

☐ 5. Brainstorm on how to create appropriate lighting effects.

☐ 6. Learn how to use the lights to get the effects you want. Place an actor onstage and experiment with different angles and intensity.

☐ 7. Map out your lighting plan using the script.

☐ 8. Practice with the lights.

☐ 9. Keep a list of anything you borrow and return it promptly after the show.

☐ 10. Write thank-you notes to anyone who helped your committee.

## Checklist for the Set Committee

☐   1. Make a list of the name and phone number of each member of the committee.

☐   2. Read through the play and list the different scenes and how many set changes there are.

☐   3. Brainstorm about what you would like to do for each scene.

☐   4. Meet with the director to go over ideas and make decisions.

☐   5. Make a list of materials and tools you will need. Estimate the cost.

☐   6. Get permission to purchase the materials, and have everything you need for each work period.

☐   7. Agree on a construction schedule. Remember to give yourselves an extra hour for each work period to enable enough time for setup and cleanup.

☐   8. Organize each work period so that each person on the committee has a job.

☐   9. Make a list of all the steps required for the completion of each set.

☐  10. Keep your work areas clean and orderly.

☐  11. Keep a list of anything you borrow and return it promptly after the show.

☐  12. Write thank-you notes to anyone who helped your committee.

## Checklist for the Costume Committee

☐ 1. Make a list of the name and phone number of each member of the committee.

☐ 2. List all the characters in the play and how many costume changes each has.

☐ 3. Meet with the director and brainstorm ideas.

☐ 4. List ideas for each character.

☐ 5. Be creative and resourceful; consider how much the cast can help.

☐ 6. Assign responsibility for specific costumes to each committee member.

☐ 7. Schedule times when you can go to secondhand clothing stores.

☐ 8. Get permission to purchase costumes or fabric.

☐ 9. Purchase a garment rack.

☐ 10. As you gather costumes, make a bag with each actor's name on it and keep the carefully folded costumes in the bags. Keep notes written on each bag of any work that needs to be done.

☐ 11. Expect to make changes to costumes after the first dress rehearsal. Do not be discouraged; making adjustments along the way is part of costuming.

☐ 12. During the course of the performances, remember to have an iron and ironing board set up in the changing room.

☐ 13. Keep a list of anything you borrow and make sure you clean it and return it promptly after the show.

☐ 14. Write thank-you notes to anyone who helped your committee.

## Checklist for the Prop Committee

☐  1. Make a list of the name and phone number of each member of the committee.

☐  2. Read through the play and make a list of all the props needed for the play. Do this carefully.

☐  3. Brainstorm about where you can get the props or how you can make them.

☐  4. Meet with the director to go over all your ideas.

☐  5. Create a budget and get permission to purchase props or materials to make them.

☐  6. Give each student responsibility for a certain number of props.

☐  7. Keep a list of anything you borrow, including the owner's name and telephone number.

☐  8. Set up the prop table scene by scene.

☐  9. Promptly return anything you borrowed with a thank-you note.

☐  10. Write thank-you notes to anyone who helped the prop committee.

## Checklist for the Publicity Committee

☐  1. Make a list of the name and phone number of each member of the committee.

☐  2. Read through the play and get a general idea about the story.

☐  3. Meet with the director and brainstorm about a unified theme for all your publicity, and how to make posters, tickets, and programs.

☐  4. Schedule a time for creating each item or assign each person on the committee to be in charge of one item.

☐  5. Make a list of all materials and tools needed and create a budget.

☐  6. Get permission to purchase materials.

☐  7. Write articles/press releases for newspapers, create ads, schedule any interviews.

☐  8. Distribute posters and assign one person to be in charge of ticket sales.

☐  9. Write the program. Be sure you haven't forgotten anyone. Have an adult proofread it.

☐  10. Sell ads to help pay printing costs.

☐  11. Get the program printed the week before the show.

☐  12. Write thank-you notes to anyone who helped the committee.

# Resources

## Recommended Books and Audiotapes

Corson, Richard. 1981. *Stage Makeup*. Englewood Cliffs, NJ: Prentice Hall.

Evans, Cheryl, and Lucy Smith. 1992. *Acting and Theater*. Tulsa, OK: EDC.

Hoggett, Chris. 1975. *Stage Crafts*. New York: St. Martin's.

Kent, Corita, and Jan Stewart. 1992. *Learning by Heart: Teachings to Free the Creative Spirit*. New York: Bantam.

Kohl, Herbert R. 1988. *Making Theater*. New York: Teachers and Writers Collaborative.

Loeschike, Maravene Sheppard. 1982. *All About Mime*. Englewood Cliffs, NJ: Prentice Hall.

Nelms, Henning. 1975. *Scene Design: A Guide to the Stage*. New York: Dover.

Phaidon Theater Manuals. *Costume and Makeup* by Michael Holt (1995); *Directing a Play* by Michael McCaffery (1995); *Stage Design* by Michael Holt (1995); *Stage Management and Theater Administration* by Pauline Menear and Terry Hawkins (1995). New York: Phaidon.

Vocal Power Institute. *Born to Sing*. Four cassette tapes and instruction book. (*Address:* 18653 Ventura Blvd., Suite #551, Tarzana, CA 91356. *Phone:* 818-895-SING.)

## Catalogs for Ordering Plays and Musicals

Baker's Plays (*Address:* P.O. Box 69922, Quincy, MA 02269. *Phone:* 617-745-0805.)

Dramatists Play Service (*Address:* 440 Park Avenue South, New York, NY 10016. *Phone:* 212-683-8960. *Web site:* postmaster @dramatists.com.)

I. E. Clark Publications (*Address:* P.O. Box 246, Schuelenburg, TX 78956-0246. *Phone:* 409-743-3232.)

Tams-Witmark Music Library, Inc. (*Address:* 560 Lexington Avenue, New York, NY 10022. *Phone:* 212-688-2525.)

## Shakespeare

The New Folger Library series of Shakespearean plays is available through most bookstores. These paperback editions are an excellent resource for students in reading the Bard's work. The more difficult words or phrases are defined on each page, making the written material more accessible for the beginning student. I highly recommend this series, as the paperbacks are affordable (the last one I bought was $3.99) and you'll not find a more comprehensive edition for the price. Published by Pocket Books, a division of Simon and Schuster, 1230 Avenue of the Americas, New York, NY 10020.

The Folger Shakespeare Library in Washington, D.C., is a research library dedicated to the works of Shakespeare and the civilization of early modern Europe. It offers a wide selection of educational programs and services.

*Shakespeare: A Magazine for Teachers and Enthusiasts* is a gem of a publication if you are teaching Shakespeare or are interested in learning more about his work. There are three issues per year: fall, winter, and spring. Sponsored by Cambridge University Press and Georgetown University. (*Address:* Georgetown University, P.O. Box 571006, Washington, D.C., 20057-1006. *Web site:* www.shakespearemag.com.)

*The Shakespeare Catalog* lists hundreds of materials to help teach Shakespeare. (*Address:* The Writing Company, 10200 Jefferson Blvd., P.O. Box 802, Culver City, CA 90232-0802. *Phone:* 800-421-4246.)

## Original Stage Adaptations
## by Jan Helling Croteau

For information concerning these stage adaptations please write to Jan Helling Croteau, Stage Adaptations, Union Wharf Road, Tuftonboro, NH 03816.

*Romeo and Juliet.* Edited stage adaptation. Set during the American Civil War, this adaptation is narrated by a stage character named Matthew Brady (the famous Civil War photographer and newspaper correspondent). All the original language is intact. The lines have been edited for length only. There are suggestions for staging, as well as production ideas. It is excellent for high school productions or homeschooled groups. This is the Encore Young People's Stage Company's most popular play; audiences loved it! (Length: approximately two hours.)

*As You Like It.* Edited stage adaptation. Set during Elizabethan times, this adaptation has been edited in length with the addition of narrators, who are the three main characters, as old people reminiscing about the story of their early years. Original score (piano sheet music) by composer Julie Way has been added. The audience raved about this comedy and it was a big hit when it was performed for elementary school and middle and high school audiences. (Length: approximately ninety minutes.)

*Twelfth Night.* Edited stage adaptation. Set during the late 1930s, in the swing-dance era. The eight narrators are maids from each of the houses who come in and out of the scenes to narrate the story. This hilarious comedy has been adapted into a musical; composer Julie Way wrote the music and lyrics. There are suggestions for choreography, and stage directions. This was our most recent production and was such a hit that many people returned to see it a second time during its running. (Length: approximately two hours.)

# About the Author

Jan Helling Croteau, of Center Tuftonboro, New Hamsphire, founded Encore Young People's Stage Company in 1994 to encourage and serve the interests of students in all areas of theatrical production and performance. She has directed six original stage adaptations of Shakespearean plays for the locally renowned Encore troupe of forty students ages six to eighteen. She has also taught drama to local public school students, and in 1996 she received the Governor Wentworth Arts Council Scholarship to teach local students mask-making techniques for stage performance.

Her passion for theatre evolved from two primary sources: as a professional fine artist who has used various mediums for exploring creative potential and as a homeschooling parent for both her own children and the local collective of homeschoolers for the past eighteen years. In this capacity she has taught many subjects including history, fine art, writing, and literature.

Jan Croteau cofounded the Young Women's Oral History Project, which was funded by grants from local civic organizations and recognized by several state historical societies. The project involved instructing students in how to conduct oral history interviews, which she then crafted into a dramatization that was performed for historical societies and general audiences throughout the state. In 1997 she set up a theatre apprenticeship program to teach older teens how to direct and produce plays with elementary and junior high students.

Jan has drawn upon the knowledge and skills gained as a children's theatre director to offer *Perform It! The Complete Guide to Directing Young People's Theatre* so that others may embark on the sort of successful and soul-satisfying experiences she has had with the Encore Young People's Stage Company.